The Science-Backed Dash Diet Cookbook for Beginners

100+ Heart-Healthy Recipes to Lower Your Blood Pressure - Includes 30-Day Meal Plan, Shopping List and Colored Pictures

GET YOUR FREE EXCLUSIVE BONUSES NOW!

DOWNLOAD FOR FREE — SIMPLY SCAN THE QR CODE BELOW!

 **30 DAY MEAL PLAN**

 **SHOPPING LIST**

 **FREE MEDITERRANEAN DIET RECIPE E-BOOK**

SCAN ME

Contents

Introduction to the DASH Diet...7
The Core Principles of the DASH Diet 8

Breakfast Recipes 10
Oatmeal with Berries & Almonds...11
Greek Yogurt with Nuts & Honey 12
Avocado Toast with Egg on Whole-Wheat Bread 13
Banana & Chia Seed Breakfast Bowl..14
Scrambled Egg Whites with Spinach & Feta 15
Whole-Wheat Pancakes with Fresh Berries.........................16
Cottage Cheese with Walnuts & Cinnamon.........................17
Vegetable & Cheese Omelet...18
Peanut Butter & Banana on Whole-Grain Toast................19
Sweet Potato & Black Bean Breakfast Hash.........................20
Quinoa Breakfast Bowl with Almonds & Raisins 21
Low-Sodium Breakfast Burrito (Egg, Avocado & Beans)...22
Whole-Grain English Muffin with Almond Butter..............23
High-Protein Chia Pudding with Nuts & Seeds 24
Tomato & Basil Scrambled Eggs on Whole-Wheat Toast..25
Spinach & Mushroom Breakfast Wrap 26
Oatmeal with Flaxseeds & Cinnamon.....................................27
Baked Apple Oatmeal Bars 28
Hard-Boiled Eggs with Whole-Grain Crackers 29
Zucchini & Cheese Breakfast Muffins 30

Lunch Recipes.. 31
Grilled Chicken Salad with Olive Oil Dressing....................32
Lentil & Chickpea Power Bowl..33
Quinoa & Black Bean Salad with Lime Dressing 34
Turkey & Spinach Whole-Wheat Wrap 35
Mediterranean Chickpea & Feta Salad....................................36
Baked Salmon with Roasted Vegetables................................37
Grilled Shrimp with Brown Rice & Steamed Broccoli......38
Egg Salad on Whole-Grain Toast (Low Mayo) 39
Hummus & Roasted Veggie Pita Pocket 40
Spinach & Grilled Chicken Stuffed Sweet Potato..............41
Brown Rice & Grilled Tofu Stir-Fry..42
Avocado & Turkey Lettuce Wraps..43
Lemon Herb Baked Cod with Asparagus................................44
Whole-Wheat Pasta with Roasted Vegetables & Feta......45
Balsamic Glazed Chicken with Roasted Brussels Sprouts....46

Stuffed Bell Peppers with Ground Turkey & Quinoa..................................47
Grilled Veggie & Hummus Whole-Wheat Wrap 48
Spiced Lentil & Roasted Cauliflower Bowl 49
Zucchini Noodles with Pesto & Grilled Chicken 50

Dinner Recipes 51
Grilled Chicken with Roasted Sweet Potatoes 52
Stir-Fried Tofu with Brown Rice & Vegetables 53
Baked Cod with Lemon & Garlic 54
Turkey Chili with Black Beans & Avocado 55
Mediterranean-Style Stuffed Peppers 56
Balsamic Glazed Salmon with Steamed Green Beans 57
Quinoa-Stuffed Eggplant with Herbs & Parmesan 58
Low-Sodium Herb Roasted Chicken with Quinoa Pilaf 59
Garlic & Lime Shrimp with Whole-Wheat Couscous 60
Whole-Wheat Pasta with Spinach, Olive Oil & Garlic 61
Lean Beef Stir-Fry with Brown Rice & Peppers 62
Grilled Pork Tenderloin with Mashed Cauliflower 63
Sweet Potato & Black Bean Enchiladas (Low-Sodium) 64
Roasted Chicken with Roasted Vegetables 65
Tofu & Broccoli Stir-Fry with Cashews 66
Grilled Salmon with Mango Salsa & Brown Rice 67
Turkey Meatballs with Whole-Wheat Spaghetti 68
Stuffed Acorn Squash with Wild Rice & Nuts 69
Roasted Brussels Sprouts & Quinoa with Almonds 70
Baked Tilapia with Garlic & Roasted Carrots 71

Soups & Stews.. 72
Hearty Vegetable Soup with Lentils..73
Low-Sodium Minestrone with Whole-Grain Pasta 74
Tomato Basil Soup with Quinoa...75
Lentil & Kale Stew with Garlic & Herbs...76
Chicken & Brown Rice Soup (Low-Sodium) 77
Spiced Sweet Potato & Carrot Soup 78
Mediterranean Chickpea & Spinach Stew 79
Roasted Red Pepper & Tomato Soup..80
Quinoa & Black Bean Chili soup 81
Coconut Curry Lentil Soup..82

Snacks & Sides.. 83
Hummus with Carrot & Cucumber Sticks 84
Handful of Unsalted Almonds & Walnuts 85
Apple Slices with Peanut Butter 86

Low-Fat Cottage Cheese with Blueberries...87
Roasted Chickpeas with Smoked Paprika 88
Baked Sweet Potato Fries with Garlic & Herbs.......................................89
Whole-Wheat Crackers with Avocado & Feta..90
Greek Yogurt with Cinnamon & Flaxseeds 91
Cucumber Slices with Hummus & Cherry Tomatoes 92
Hard-Boiled Eggs with Whole-Grain Crackers 93

Smoothies & Drinks 94
Green Smoothie with Spinach, Banana & Almond Milk 95
Berry & Chia Protein Smoothie 96
Low-Sodium Tomato Juice Blend 97
Cucumber & Mint Hydration Drink..98
Almond Butter & Banana Smoothie 99
Strawberry & Flaxseed Yogurt Smoothie...100
Watermelon & Coconut Water Refresher 101
Low-Sugar Almond Milk Latte..102
Pineapple & Ginger Immunity Boost Smoothie....................................103
Turmeric Golden Milk with Almond Milk 104

Desserts 105
Dark Chocolate Avocado Mousse...106
Chia Seed Pudding with Almond Milk & Berries 107
Oatmeal & Berry Crumble (Low Sugar) 108
Baked Apple with Cinnamon & Walnuts 109
Banana & Walnut Energy Bites...110
Greek Yogurt with Honey & Pistachios 111
Low-Sugar Almond Flour Brownies 112
Frozen Banana & Peanut Butter Bites 113
Coconut & Chia Seed Pudding with Mango..114
Baked Peaches with Almond Butter Drizzle..115

30-Day Diet Meal Plan & Shopping List 116
Week 1...116
Week 2...118
Week 3...120
Week 4...122

Index...124

INTRODUCTION TO THE DASH DIET

For decades, high blood pressure—also known as hypertension—has been a silent yet deadly health concern affecting millions worldwide. Often referred to as the "silent killer," hypertension gradually increases the risk of heart disease, stroke, and kidney failure. While medications are widely prescribed, experts have long sought a natural, long-term solution. This search led to one of the most scientifically-backed and effective eating plans available today: the DASH Diet.

What is the DASH Diet?

The Dietary Approaches to Stop Hypertension (DASH) Diet is more than just a meal plan—it's a scientifically proven approach to improving heart health and overall well-being. Unlike restrictive fad diets, DASH focuses on balance, variety, and moderation, emphasizing nutrient-rich foods that naturally support healthy blood pressure levels.

At its core, the DASH Diet promotes:
- **Whole, unprocessed foods** such as fruits, vegetables, whole grains, lean proteins, and low-fat dairy.
- **Heart-healthy nutrients**, particularly potassium, calcium, and magnesium, which help regulate blood pressure.
- **Reduced sodium intake,** encouraging flavorful cooking with herbs, spices, and natural seasonings instead of excess salt.
- **Healthy fats,** like those found in nuts, seeds, and olive oil, while limiting trans fats and processed foods.

This approach is not only effective for reducing high blood pressure but also beneficial for weight management, diabetes prevention, and overall cardiovascular health. It's an adaptable, long-term eating pattern designed to fit into everyday life, making it a sustainable choice for individuals and families alike.

The Origins of the DASH Diet

The DASH Diet was developed in the 1990s by the National Institutes of Health (NIH) as part of an extensive effort to combat high blood pressure through dietary changes. Researchers recognized that traditional Western diets, high in sodium, unhealthy fats, and refined sugars, contributed to the growing epidemic of hypertension and heart disease.

In response, the NIH conducted a series of groundbreaking studies to determine whether dietary changes alone could naturally lower blood pressure—without relying solely on medication. The results were remarkable.

The initial DASH study, published in 1997 in the New England Journal of Medicine, revealed that participants who followed a diet rich in fruits, vegetables, whole grains, and lean proteins saw significant reductions in blood pressure—within just a few weeks. Even more impressive, these improvements were achieved without requiring major lifestyle overhauls or strict calorie restrictions.

THE CORE PRINCIPLES OF THE DASH DIET

The DASH Diet (Dietary Approaches to Stop Hypertension) is not just about lowering blood pressure—it's about nourishing your body with the right balance of nutrients to support overall health. Unlike many restrictive diets that focus on eliminating food groups, the DASH Diet promotes a holistic and sustainable approach to eating. At the heart of the DASH Diet are four key principles:

- Focusing on whole, nutrient-dense foods
- Reducing sodium intake while maintaining flavor
- Achieving a balance of macronutrients (protein, carbohydrates, and healthy fats)
- Prioritizing fiber-rich foods for heart health

By incorporating these principles into your daily routine, you can improve heart health, support weight management, stabilize blood sugar levels, and boost overall well-being—all while enjoying a variety of flavorful and satisfying meals.

Focus on Whole, Nutrient-Dense Foods

The foundation of the DASH Diet is whole, minimally processed foods that are rich in vitamins, minerals, and antioxidants. These foods provide the essential nutrients needed to lower blood pressure, reduce inflammation, and support a healthy metabolism.

Key Food Groups in the DASH Diet:

Fruits and Vegetables – Packed with potassium, magnesium, and fiber, which naturally help regulate blood pressure.

Whole Grains – A great source of complex carbohydrates and fiber, promoting heart health and steady energy levels.

Lean Proteins – Essential for muscle repair and metabolism, with a focus on lean meats, poultry, fish, beans, and plant-based sources.

Low-Fat Dairy – Provides calcium and protein, which are important for bone strength and heart function.

Healthy Fats – Found in nuts, seeds, avocados, and olive oil, these fats help support brain function and reduce inflammation.

What to Minimize:

While the DASH Diet is not overly restrictive, it encourages limiting:

- Processed foods that contain added sugars, unhealthy fats, and excess sodium.
- Refined carbohydrates like white bread, pastries, and sugary cereals.
- Sugary beverages such as sodas, energy drinks, and fruit juices with added sugar.
- High-fat dairy and red meats (instead, opt for leaner protein sources).

By choosing whole foods over processed options, you naturally increase your intake of heart-healthy nutrients while reducing harmful additives that can contribute to hypertension and chronic disease.

Balance of Macronutrients (Protein, Carbs, Healthy Fats)

A balanced diet isn't just about what foods you eat—it's also about how those foods work together to fuel your body. The DASH Diet encourages an optimal balance of macronutrients—proteins, carbohydrates, and healthy fats—to support energy levels, satiety, and overall well-being.

Protein:
Why it matters: Supports muscle growth, metabolism, and blood sugar stability.

Best DASH-approved sources:
- Lean meats (chicken, turkey, fish)
- Plant-based proteins (beans, lentils, tofu, quinoa)
- Nuts and seeds (almonds, walnuts, flaxseeds)
- Low-fat dairy (Greek yogurt, cottage cheese)

Carbohydrates:
Why they matter: Provide essential energy for daily activities and brain function.

Best DASH-approved sources:
- Whole grains (quinoa, brown rice, whole-wheat pasta)
- Starchy vegetables (sweet potatoes, squash, carrots)
- Fiber-rich fruits (berries, apples, pears)

Healthy Fats:
Why they matter: Support heart health, brain function, and inflammation reduction.

Best DASH-approved sources:
- Avocados
- Olive oil
- Fatty fish (salmon, mackerel, tuna)
- Nuts and seeds (chia seeds, flaxseeds, walnuts)

Balancing protein, healthy fats, and fiber-rich carbs helps regulate blood sugar, reduce cravings, and maintain steady energy throughout the day.

BREAKFAST RECIPES

OATMEAL WITH BERRIES & ALMONDS

 PREP TIME:
5 MINS

 COOK TIME:
10 MINS

 SERVING:
2

INGREDIENTS

1 cup rolled oats
2 cups unsweetened almond milk
½ teaspoon cinnamon
1 teaspoon honey (optional)

½ cup mixed berries (blueberries, raspberries, strawberries)
2 tablespoons sliced almonds

INSTRUCTIONS

1. Get a small saucepan and add the milk, oats, and cinnamon.
2. Cook on moderate heat, stirring occasionally, for about 8–10 minutes, until the oats soften and absorb most of the liquid.
3. Remove from heat, then ladle the oatmeal into bowls. Toss in the fresh berries and drizzle with honey if desired.
4. Sprinkle chopped almonds on top and serve warm.

Nutritional Values (per serving): Calories: 230 | Total Carbs: 38g | Net Carbs: 34g | Sugar: 7g | Protein: 8g | Fat: 6g | Saturated Fat: 1g | Cholesterol: 5mg | Sodium: 60mg

GREEK YOGURT WITH NUTS & HONEY

 PREP TIME: 5 MINS   **COOK TIME:** 00 MINS   **SERVING:** 2

INGREDIENTS

1 ½ cups Greek yogurt (low-fat or non-fat)
2 tablespoons chopped walnuts or almonds
1 teaspoon honey

½ teaspoon cinnamon
½ cup mixed berries (optional)

INSTRUCTIONS

1. Spoon the Greek yogurt evenly into two serving bowls, making sure it has a smooth surface.
2. Chop the walnuts or almonds into small pieces for an even crunch. Toss in the nuts over the yogurt, spreading them evenly across the surface.
3. Drizzle the honey over the top, letting it seep into the yogurt and coat the nuts. Sprinkle the cinnamon lightly over everything for extra warmth and flavor.
4. Add fresh berries on top if desired for a burst of color and sweetness. Serve immediately or refrigerate for a chilled breakfast.

Nutritional Values (per serving): Calories: 180 | Total Carbs: 18g | Net Carbs: 16g | Sugar: 12g | Protein: 15g | Fat: 6g | Saturated Fat: 2g | Cholesterol: 10mg | Sodium: 50mg

AVOCADO TOAST WITH EGG ON WHOLE-WHEAT BREAD

 PREP TIME: 5 MINS

 COOK TIME: 5 MINS

 SERVING: 2

INGREDIENTS

2 slices whole-wheat bread
1 ripe avocado
2 large eggs
½ teaspoon lemon juice
¼ teaspoon black pepper
¼ teaspoon sea salt

INSTRUCTIONS

1. Place the slices of whole-wheat bread in a toaster and toast until it turns golden brown and crisp on both. Cut the avocado in half to remove the pit, and scoop the flesh into a deep-bottom bowl.
2. Mash the avocado until smooth but slightly chunky. Mix in the lemon juice, salt, and crushed pepper.
3. Heat a non-stick skillet on moderate heat and lightly coat it with 1/2 tsp oil or cooking spray.
4. Crack the eggs into the pan and cook for 2–3 minutes.
5. Spread the mashed avocado evenly over the toasted bread slices, ensuring full coverage. Carefully place one cooked egg on top of each slice.
6. Serve immediately while warm, with extra black pepper or red pepper flakes if desired.

Nutritional Values (per serving):   Calories: 250 | Total Carbs: 22g | Net Carbs: 18g | Sugar: 3g | Protein: 10g |

Fat: 14g | Saturated Fat: 3g | Cholesterol: 185mg | Sodium: 220mg

BANANA & CHIA SEED BREAKFAST BOWL

 PREP TIME: 5 MINS   **COOK TIME:** 00 MINS   **SERVING:** 2

INGREDIENTS

1 banana, sliced
1 cup Greek yogurt (low-fat or non-fat)
1 tablespoon chia seeds
½ teaspoon cinnamon
1 teaspoon honey (optional)

2 tablespoons granola (low-sugar)

INSTRUCTIONS

1. Slice the banana into even rounds and set aside. Divide the Greek yogurt evenly between two bowls, creating a smooth base.
2. Sprinkle the chia seeds over the yogurt, allowing them to absorb moisture and expand slightly. Toss in the banana slices, arranging them evenly across the yogurt.
3. If using, drizzle the honey over the top, adding natural sweetness to balance the flavors. Sprinkle cinnamon for an aromatic touch, ensuring even distribution.
4. Finish with a layer of granola for a satisfying crunch.
5. Serve immediately, or let it sit for a few minutes to soften the chia seeds.

Nutritional Values (per serving):   Calories: 220 | Total Carbs: 36g | Net Carbs: 31g | Sugar: 14g | Protein: 12g | Fat: 5g | Saturated Fat: 1g | Cholesterol: 5mg | Sodium: 40mg

SCRAMBLED EGG WHITES WITH SPINACH & FETA

 PREP TIME: 5 MINS   **COOK TIME:** 5 MINS   **SERVING:** 2

INGREDIENTS

4 large egg whites
1 teaspoon olive oil
1 cup fresh spinach, chopped
¼ cup crumbled feta cheese
¼ teaspoon black pepper
⅛ teaspoon sea salt

INSTRUCTIONS

1. Heat one tsp oil in a non-stick skillet on moderate heat. Toss in the chopped spinach and sauté for 1–2 minutes, until wilted.
2. Grab a shallow bowl and whisk the egg whites with salt and black pepper until frothy. Ladle egg whites into the skillet and gently stir with a spatula.
3. Cook for 2–3 minutes, stirring occasionally, until the eggs are soft and set. Spread crumbled feta cheese over the eggs and cook for 30 seconds more.
4. Serve immediately, pairing with whole-grain toast or fresh fruit.

Nutritional Values (per serving): Calories: 130 | Total Carbs: 3g | Net Carbs: 2g | Sugar: 1g | Protein: 15g | Fat: 5g | Saturated Fat: 2g | Cholesterol: 15mg | Sodium: 190mg

WHOLE-WHEAT PANCAKES WITH FRESH BERRIES

 PREP TIME: 5 MINS

 COOK TIME: 10 MINS

 SERVING: 2

INGREDIENTS

½ cup whole-wheat flour
½ teaspoon baking powder
1 teaspoon cinnamon
½ cup low-fat milk or almond milk
1 large egg
1 teaspoon honey

½ teaspoon vanilla extract
½ cup fresh mixed berries
1 teaspoon olive oil (for cooking)

INSTRUCTIONS

1. Grab the shallow bowl and whisk together the whole-wheat flour, baking powder, and cinnamon. In another bowl, beat the egg, milk, honey, and vanilla extract until smooth.
2. Combine the wet and dry elements mixture, stirring until just mixed (avoid over-mixing). Heat a non-stick skillet on moderate heat and coat with olive oil.
3. Spoon small amounts of batter onto the skillet to form pancakes. Cook for 2–3 minutes, then flip and cook more for 2 minutes.
4. Serve warm with fresh berries on top and a drizzle of honey if desired.

Nutritional Values (per serving): Calories: 210 | Total Carbs: 35g | Net Carbs: 30g | Sugar: 8g | Protein: 8g |

Fat: 6g | Saturated Fat: 1g | Cholesterol: 60mg | Sodium: 180mg

COTTAGE CHEESE WITH WALNUTS & CINNAMON

 PREP TIME:
5 MINS

 COOK TIME:
00 MINS

 SERVING:
2

INGREDIENTS

1 cup low-fat cottage cheese
2 tablespoons walnuts, chopped
½ teaspoon cinnamon
1 teaspoon honey (optional)

INSTRUCTIONS

1. Divide the cottage cheese into two serving bowls. Chop the walnuts into small pieces for an even crunch.
2. Sprinkle the walnuts and cinnamon over the cottage cheese. If you want a touch of sweetness, drizzle honey over the top.
3. Serve immediately.

Nutritional Values (per serving): Calories: 160 | Total Carbs: 12g | Net Carbs: 10g | Sugar: 6g | Protein: 14g |

Fat: 6g | Saturated Fat: 2g | Cholesterol: 15mg | Sodium: 180mg

VEGETABLE & CHEESE OMELET

 PREP TIME: 5 MINS

 COOK TIME: 7 MINS

 SERVING: 2

INGREDIENTS

3 large eggs
½ cup bell peppers, diced
¼ cup mushrooms, sliced
¼ cup low-fat shredded cheese
1 teaspoon olive oil
¼ teaspoon black pepper

⅛ teaspoon sea salt

INSTRUCTIONS

1. Grab a shallow bowl and whisk the eggs with salt and black pepper until fluffy. Heat one tsp oil in a non-stick skillet on moderate heat.
2. Sauté the diced bell peppers and mushrooms for 2 minutes, until tender. Ladle beaten eggs over the veggies, tilting the pan for even coverage.
3. Cook for 3–4 minutes, occasionally lifting the edges to allow uncooked egg to flow underneath.
4. Sprinkle the shredded cheese on one side of the omelet. Fold the omelet and cook for 30 seconds, then serve warm.

Nutritional Values (per serving): Calories: 200 | Total Carbs: 8g | Net Carbs: 6g | Sugar: 3g | Protein: 15g |

Fat: 12g | Saturated Fat: 4g | Cholesterol: 240mg | Sodium: 210mg

PEANUT BUTTER & BANANA ON WHOLE-GRAIN TOAST

 **PREP TIME:**
5 MINS

 COOK TIME:
00 MINS

 SERVING:
2

INGREDIENTS

2 slices whole-grain bread
2 tablespoons natural peanut
butter
1 banana, sliced
¼ teaspoon cinnamon

INSTRUCTIONS

1. Toast the whole-grain bread slices until golden brown. Spread one tbsp of peanut butter on each slice.
2. Arrange banana slices and smooth over the peanut butter. Sprinkle cinnamon over the top for added flavor.
3. Serve immediately as a satisfying and energy-packed breakfast.

Nutritional Values (per serving): Calories: 280 | Total Carbs: 38g | Net Carbs: 34g | Sugar: 10g | Protein: 10g
| Fat: 12g | Saturated Fat: 2g | Cholesterol: 0mg | Sodium: 150mg

SWEET POTATO & BLACK BEAN BREAKFAST HASH

 PREP TIME:
5 MINS

 COOK TIME:
10 MINS

 SERVING:
2

INGREDIENTS

1 medium sweet potato, diced
½ cup black beans drained and rinsed
½ teaspoon cumin
¼ teaspoon smoked paprika
1 teaspoon olive oil

¼ teaspoon black pepper
⅛ teaspoon sea salt

INSTRUCTIONS

1. Heat one tsp oil in a skillet on moderate heat. Toss in the diced sweet potatoes and sauté for 6–7 minutes, stirring occasionally.
2. Add black beans, cumin, smoked paprika, black pepper, and salt. Cook for another 3–4 minutes, stirring until the flavors meld.
3. Serve warm, optionally topped with fresh cilantro or a fried egg.

Nutritional Values (per serving): Calories: 230 | Total Carbs: 40g | Net Carbs: 35g | Sugar: 7g | Protein: 7g | Fat: 5g | Saturated Fat: 1g | Cholesterol: 0mg | Sodium: 160mg

QUINOA BREAKFAST BOWL WITH ALMONDS & RAISINS

 PREP TIME: 5 MINS

 COOK TIME: 10 MINS

 SERVING: 2

INGREDIENTS

½ cup quinoa, rinsed
1 cup almond milk or low-fat milk
1 tablespoon raisins
1 tablespoon sliced almonds
½ teaspoon cinnamon
1 teaspoon honey (optional)

INSTRUCTIONS

1. In a small pot, get the almond milk to a gentle simmer. Toss in the rinsed quinoa and cook for 10 minutes, until tender.
2. Stir in the raisins and cinnamon, letting the flavors blend. Ladle the mixture into serving bowls, sprinkle with sliced almonds, and drizzle sweetener if desired.
3. Serve warm and enjoy a protein-packed start to the day.

Nutritional Values (per serving): Macros: Protein 8% / Fat 23% / Carbs 69% | Calories: 230 | Total carbs: 38g
| Net carbs: 34g | Sugar: 10g | Protein: 8g | Fat: 6g | Saturated fat: 1g | Cholesterol: 0mg | Sodium: 80mg

LOW-SODIUM BREAKFAST BURRITO (EGG, AVOCADO & BEANS)

 **PREP TIME:** 5 MINS

 COOK TIME: 10 MINS

 SERVING: 2

INGREDIENTS

2 whole-wheat tortillas
4 large eggs
½ cup black beans drained and rinsed
½ avocado, sliced
¼ cup shredded low-fat cheese

¼ teaspoon black pepper
⅛ teaspoon sea salt
1 teaspoon olive oil

INSTRUCTIONS

1. Heat one tsp oil in a non-stick skillet on moderate heat, then whisk and cook the eggs with salt and black pepper until soft and fluffy.
2. Warm the whole-wheat tortillas in a dry pan for 30 seconds per side, then spread the black beans evenly on each tortilla.
3. Top with scrambled eggs, sprinkle shredded cheese and add avocado slices.
4. Fold and roll into a burrito, then serve warm with fresh salsa or sliced veggies.

Nutritional Values (per serving): Calories: 230 | Total carbs: 38g | Net carbs: 34g | Sugar: 10g | Protein: 8g |

Fat: 6g | Saturated fat: 1g | Cholesterol: 0mg | Sodium: 80mg

WHOLE-GRAIN ENGLISH MUFFIN WITH ALMOND BUTTER

 PREP TIME:
5 MINS

 COOK TIME:
00 MINS

 SERVING:
2

INGREDIENTS

2 whole-grain English muffins,
split
2 tablespoons almond butter
½ teaspoon cinnamon
1 teaspoon honey (optional)

INSTRUCTIONS

1. Toast the English muffin halves until golden brown and crisp.
2. Spread 1 tablespoon of almond butter evenly over each half.
3. Sprinkle cinnamon over the top and drizzle with honey if desired.
4. Serve immediately, paired with fresh fruit or yogurt, for a complete breakfast.

Nutritional Values (per serving):   Carbs 69% | Calories: 230 | Total carbs: 38g | Net carbs: 34g | Sugar: 10g |

Protein: 8g | Fat: 6g | Saturated fat: 1g | Cholesterol: 0mg | Sodium: 80mg

HIGH-PROTEIN CHIA PUDDING WITH NUTS & SEEDS

PREP TIME: 5 MINS

COOK TIME: 00 MINS

SERVING: 2

INGREDIENTS

½ cup unsweetened almond milk
¼ cup Greek yogurt (low-fat)
2 tablespoons chia seeds
1 teaspoon honey (optional)
1 tablespoon mixed nuts
(almonds, walnuts, or pecans)

1 teaspoon flaxseeds

INSTRUCTIONS

1. Whisk together almond milk, Greek yogurt, and chia seeds in a deep-bottom bowl and then stir in honey if using.
2. Cover and refrigerate for 4 hours (at least) or overnight, allowing the chia seeds to expand.
3. Stir well before serving and sprinkle with mixed nuts and flaxseeds.
4. Enjoy chilled as a creamy, protein-rich breakfast option.

Nutritional Values (per serving): Macros: Protein 8% / Fat 23% / Carbs 69% | Calories: 230 | Total carbs: 38g

| Net carbs: 34g | Sugar: 10g | Protein: 8g | Fat: 6g | Saturated fat: 1g | Cholesterol: 0mg | Sodium: 80mg

TOMATO & BASIL SCRAMBLED EGGS ON WHOLE-WHEAT TOAST

 PREP TIME: 5 MINS

 COOK TIME: 5 MINS

 SERVING: 2

INGREDIENTS

4 large eggs
1 teaspoon olive oil
½ cup cherry tomatoes, halved
¼ teaspoon black pepper
⅛ teaspoon sea salt
4 basil leaves, chopped

2 slices whole-wheat bread, toasted

INSTRUCTIONS

1. Heat one tsp oil in a non-stick skillet on moderate heat, then sauté cherry tomatoes for 1–2 minutes until softened.
2. Whisk and cook eggs with salt and pepper in the pan, stirring for 3 minutes until soft.
3. Stir in chopped basil, then spoon the scrambled eggs over toasted whole-wheat bread.
4. Serve immediately; spread extra basil on top if desired.

Nutritional Values (per serving): Macros: Protein 8% / Fat 23% / Carbs 69% | Calories: 230 | Total carbs: 38g
| Net carbs: 34g | Sugar: 10g | Protein: 8g | Fat: 6g | Saturated fat: 1g | Cholesterol: 0mg | Sodium: 80mg

SPINACH & MUSHROOM BREAKFAST WRAP

 PREP TIME: 5 MINS

 COOK TIME: 7 MINS

 SERVING: 2

INGREDIENTS

2 whole-wheat tortillas
4 large eggs
½ cup mushrooms, sliced
1 cup fresh spinach
1 teaspoon olive oil
¼ cup low-fat shredded cheese

¼ teaspoon black pepper

INSTRUCTIONS

1. Heat one tsp oil in a non-stick skillet on moderate heat, then sauté mushrooms and spinach for 2–3 minutes until softened.
2. Whisk and cook eggs with black pepper, stirring for 3 minutes until fluffy.
3. Place the egg mixture onto each tortilla and sprinkle with shredded cheese.
4. Roll into a wrap and serve warm with a side of fresh fruit.

Nutritional Values (per serving): Macros: Protein 8% / Fat 23% / Carbs 69% | Calories: 230 | Total carbs: 38g
| Net carbs: 34g | Sugar: 10g | Protein: 8g | Fat: 6g | Saturated fat: 1g | Cholesterol: 0mg | Sodium: 80mg

OATMEAL WITH FLAXSEEDS & CINNAMON

 PREP TIME: 5 MINS

 COOK TIME: 10 MINS

 SERVING: 2

INGREDIENTS

1 cup rolled oats
2 cups unsweetened almond milk
½ teaspoon cinnamon
1 tablespoon flaxseeds
1 teaspoon honey (optional)

INSTRUCTIONS

1. Heat milk in a small pot, then toss in oats and cinnamon, stirring occasionally.
2. Simmer for 8–10 minutes until the oats soften and absorb most of the liquid.
3. Remove from heat and stir in flaxseeds, letting the flavors meld.
4. Ladle into bowls, drizzle with honey if desired, and serve warm.

Nutritional Values (per serving): Macros: Protein 8% / Fat 23% / Carbs 69% | Calories: 230 | Total carbs: 38g | Net carbs: 34g | Sugar: 10g | Protein: 8g | Fat: 6g | Saturated fat: 1g | Cholesterol: 0mg | Sodium: 80mg

BAKED APPLE OATMEAL BARS

 PREP TIME:
10 MINS

 COOK TIME:
25 MINS

 SERVING:
6

INGREDIENTS

2 cups rolled oats
1 teaspoon cinnamon
1 teaspoon baking powder
1 cup unsweetened applesauce
½ cup low-fat milk or almond milk
1 teaspoon honey

1 teaspoon vanilla extract

INSTRUCTIONS

1. Preheat oven to 350°F (175°C). Grease a baking dish.
2. Grab a shallow bowl and mix oats, cinnamon, and baking powder, then stir in applesauce, milk, honey, and vanilla.
3. Spread batter evenly and bake for 25 minutes until golden and set.
4. Let cool, then cut into bars and serve as a nutritious grab-and-go breakfast.

Nutritional Values (per serving): Macros: Protein 8% / Fat 23% / Carbs 69% | Calories: 230 | Total carbs: 38g | Net carbs: 34g | Sugar: 10g | Protein: 8g | Fat: 6g | Saturated fat: 1g | Cholesterol: 0mg | Sodium: 80mg

HARD-BOILED EGGS WITH WHOLE-GRAIN CRACKERS

PREP TIME: 5 MINS	COOK TIME: 10 MINS	SERVING: 2

INGREDIENTS

4 large eggs
8 whole-grain crackers
¼ teaspoon black pepper
⅛ teaspoon sea salt

INSTRUCTIONS

1. Place the eggs in a saucepan and cover it with cold water, then get it to a boil on moderate heat.
2. Once boiling, decrease the stove heat to low and let it cook for 8–10 minutes, then transfer eggs to ice water for 5 minutes.
3. Peel the eggs, slice them in half, and sprinkle with sea salt and black pepper.
4. Serve immediately with whole-grain crackers for a balanced, protein-packed breakfast.

Nutritional Values (per serving): Macros: Protein 8% / Fat 23% / Carbs 69% | Calories: 230 | Total carbs: 38g
| Net carbs: 34g | Sugar: 10g | Protein: 8g | Fat: 6g | Saturated fat: 1g | Cholesterol: 0mg | Sodium: 80mg

ZUCCHINI & CHEESE BREAKFAST MUFFINS

 PREP TIME: 10 MINS

 COOK TIME: 20 MINS

 SERVING: 4

INGREDIENTS

1 medium zucchini, grated
4 large eggs
½ cup low-fat shredded cheese
¼ cup whole-wheat flour
½ teaspoon baking powder
¼ teaspoon black pepper

1 teaspoon olive oil

INSTRUCTIONS

1. Preheat oven to 350°F (175°C). Grease a muffin tin with olive oil.
2. Grab a shallow bowl and whisk eggs, then stir in grated zucchini, shredded cheese, black pepper, whole-wheat flour, and baking powder.
3. Ladle batter into the muffin tin, filling every cup about ¾ full, then bake for 18–20 minutes until golden and set.
4. Cool slightly, then serve warm or store for a quick grab-and-go breakfast.

Nutritional Values (per serving): Macros: Protein 8% / Fat 23% / Carbs 69% | Calories: 230 | Total carbs: 38g | Net carbs: 34g | Sugar: 10g | Protein: 8g | Fat: 6g | Saturated fat: 1g | Cholesterol: 0mg | Sodium: 80mg

LUNCH RECIPES

GRILLED CHICKEN SALAD WITH OLIVE OIL DRESSING

 PREP TIME:
10 MINS

 COOK TIME:
15 MINS

 SERVING:
2

INGREDIENTS

2 boneless, skinless chicken
breasts
4 cups mixed greens (spinach,
romaine, arugula)
½ cup cherry tomatoes, halved
¼ cup sliced cucumber

¼ cup feta cheese (optional)
2 tablespoons olive oil
1 tablespoon lemon juice
¼ teaspoon black pepper
⅛ teaspoon sea salt

INSTRUCTIONS

1. Preheat a grill pan on moderate heat. Massage the chicken with 1 tablespoon olive oil, black pepper, and salt. Grill for 6–7 minutes on one side until fully cooked, then let it rest for 5 minutes before slicing.
2. Take a large deep-bottom bowl and toss the mixed greens, cherry tomatoes, cucumber, and feta cheese.
3. Whisk together the leftover oil and lemon juice to make a light dressing.
4. Arrange the sliced grilled chicken over the salad, drizzle with dressing, and serve immediately.

Nutritional Values (per serving): Calories: 340 | Total Carbs: 10g | Net Carbs: 7g | Sugar: 3g | Protein: 32g | Fat: 18g | Saturated Fat: 4g | Cholesterol: 80mg | Sodium: 260mg

LENTIL & CHICKPEA POWER BOWL

 PREP TIME:
10 MINS

 COOK TIME:
20 MINS

 SERVING:
2

INGREDIENTS

½ cup dry lentils
½ cup dry chickpeas, soaked overnight
½ cup diced cucumber
½ cup cherry tomatoes, halved
¼ cup red onion, finely chopped

2 tablespoons olive oil
1 tablespoon lemon juice
¼ teaspoon cumin
¼ teaspoon black pepper
⅛ teaspoon sea salt

INSTRUCTIONS

1. Rinse and drain the lentils and chickpeas. Boil them separately in water for 15–20 minutes until tender, then drain and let cool.
2. Grab a shallow bowl and mix the cooked lentils and chickpeas with cucumber, tomatoes, and red onion.
3. Whisk together the two tbsp oil, lemon juice, cumin, black pepper, and salt, then pour over the salad.
4. Toss well, let it sit for 5 minutes to absorb flavors, and serve fresh.

Nutritional Values (per serving): Calories: 280 | Total Carbs: 32g | Net Carbs: 28g | Sugar: 6g | Protein: 14g | Fat: 12g | Saturated Fat: 2g | Cholesterol: 0mg | Sodium: 180mg

QUINOA & BLACK BEAN SALAD WITH LIME DRESSING

 PREP TIME:
10 MINS

 COOK TIME:
15 MINS

 SERVING:
2

INGREDIENTS

½ cup dry quinoa
½ cup dry black beans soaked overnight
½ cup diced bell peppers
¼ cup red onion, finely chopped
2 tablespoons chopped cilantro

1 tablespoon olive oil
1 tablespoon fresh lime juice
¼ teaspoon black pepper
⅛ teaspoon sea salt

INSTRUCTIONS

1. Rinse and drain the quinoa, then cook in 1 cup of water on moderate heat for 15 minutes until fluffy. Let cool for 5 minutes.
2. Drain and rinse the black beans, then boil in water for 15–20 minutes until tender. Drain and set aside.
3. Mix the cooked quinoa and black beans with bell peppers, red onion, and cilantro in a deep-bottom bowl.
4. Whisk together the one tbsp oil, lime juice, black pepper, and salt, toss into the salad, and serve.

Nutritional Values (per serving): Calories: 310 | Total Carbs: 42g | Net Carbs: 36g | Sugar: 5g | Protein: 12g | Fat: 10g | Saturated Fat: 1g | Cholesterol: 0mg | Sodium: 170mg

TURKEY & SPINACH WHOLE-WHEAT WRAP

 PREP TIME: 5 MINS   **COOK TIME:** 5 MINS   **SERVING:** 2

INGREDIENTS

2 whole-wheat tortillas
6 ounces turkey breast, sliced
1 teaspoon olive oil
1 cup fresh spinach
2 tablespoons hummus
¼ teaspoon black pepper

INSTRUCTIONS

1. Heat a skillet on moderate heat, then sauté the turkey slices with olive oil and black pepper for 2–3 minutes until lightly golden.
2. Spread hummus evenly on each whole-wheat tortilla.
3. Layer the cooked turkey and fresh spinach on the tortillas, then roll tightly into a wrap.
4. Slice in half and serve immediately.

Nutritional Values (per serving): Calories: 290 | Total Carbs: 36g | Net Carbs: 30g | Sugar: 4g | Protein: 22g |

Fat: 8g | Saturated Fat: 2g | Cholesterol: 55mg | Sodium: 240mg

MEDITERRANEAN CHICKPEA & FETA SALAD

 PREP TIME:
10 MINS

 COOK TIME:
20 MINS

 SERVING:
2

INGREDIENTS

1 cup dry chickpeas, soaked overnight
½ cup diced cucumber
½ cup cherry tomatoes, halved
¼ cup crumbled feta cheese
2 tablespoons olive oil

1 tablespoon lemon juice
¼ teaspoon oregano
¼ teaspoon black pepper

INSTRUCTIONS

1. Drain and boil the chickpeas in water for 15–20 minutes until tender, then drain and let cool.
2. Grab a shallow bowl and combine chickpeas, cucumber, tomatoes, and feta cheese.
3. Whisk together the two tbsp oil, lemon juice, oregano, and black pepper, then drizzle over the salad.
4. Toss well and chill for 5 minutes before serving.

Nutritional Values (per serving): Calories: 320 | Total Carbs: 34g | Net Carbs: 28g | Sugar: 7g | Protein: 14g |
Fat: 16g | Saturated Fat: 5g | Cholesterol: 20mg | Sodium: 210mg

BAKED SALMON WITH ROASTED VEGETABLES

 **PREP TIME:**
10 MINS

 COOK TIME:
20 MINS

 SERVING:
2

INGREDIENTS

2 fresh salmon fillets (4 oz each)
1 cup broccoli florets
½ cup cherry tomatoes
1 teaspoon olive oil
¼ teaspoon black pepper
⅛ teaspoon sea salt

1 teaspoon lemon juice

INSTRUCTIONS

1. Preheat oven to 375°F (190°C). Arrange the baking sheet with parchment paper.
2. Place the salmon fillets on one side and arrange the broccoli and cherry tomatoes on the other. Drizzle everything with olive oil, then powder it with black pepper, salt, and lemon juice.
3. Bake for 15–20 minutes, until the salmon is flaky and the vegetables are tender.
4. Serve immediately, pairing with whole grains if desired.

Nutritional Values (per serving): Calories: 360 | Total Carbs: 12g | Net Carbs: 9g | Sugar: 4g | Protein: 34g |

Fat: 18g | Saturated Fat: 4g | Cholesterol: 85mg | Sodium: 220mg

GRILLED SHRIMP WITH BROWN RICE & STEAMED BROCCOLI

 PREP TIME: 10 MINS

 COOK TIME: 60 MINS

 SERVING: 2

INGREDIENTS

½ cup dry brown rice
10 large shrimp, peeled and deveined
1 teaspoon olive oil
1 teaspoon lemon juice
½ teaspoon garlic powder

1 cup broccoli florets
¼ teaspoon black pepper
⅛ teaspoon sea salt

INSTRUCTIONS

1. Cook the brown rice in one cup water for 40 minutes, until tender, then fluff with a fork and set aside.
2. Toss the shrimp with one tsp oil, lemon juice, garlic powder, crushed pepper, and salt, then grill on moderate heat for 2–3 minutes per side until pink and opaque.
3. Steam the broccoli in a pot with ½ inch of water for 3–4 minutes, then drain.
4. Serve the grilled shrimp over brown rice, with steamed broccoli on the side.

Nutritional Values (per serving): Calories: 320 | Total Carbs: 38g | Net Carbs: 32g | Sugar: 5g | Protein: 30g |

Fat: 8g | Saturated Fat: 1g | Cholesterol: 150mg | Sodium: 230mg

EGG SALAD ON WHOLE-GRAIN TOAST (LOW MAYO)

 PREP TIME: 5 MINS   **COOK TIME:** 10 MINS   **SERVING:** 2

INGREDIENTS

4 large eggs
2 tablespoons plain Greek yogurt
1 teaspoon Dijon mustard
¼ teaspoon black pepper
⅛ teaspoon sea salt
2 slices whole-grain bread

INSTRUCTIONS

1. Boil the eggs in a pot of water for 10 minutes, then transfer to ice water for 5 minutes before peeling.
2. Mash the eggs in a deep-bottom bowl and mix in Greek yogurt, Dijon mustard, black pepper, and salt until well combined.
3. Toast the whole-grain bread until golden brown.
4. Spread the egg salad evenly on the toast and serve immediately.

Nutritional Values (per serving): Calories: 280 | Total Carbs: 26g | Net Carbs: 22g | Sugar: 3g | Protein: 20g |

Fat: 12g | Saturated Fat: 3g | Cholesterol: 375mg | Sodium: 240mg

HUMMUS & ROASTED VEGGIE PITA POCKET

 PREP TIME:
10 MINS

 COOK TIME:
15 MINS

 SERVING:
2

INGREDIENTS

1 whole-wheat pita, halved
½ cup hummus
½ cup bell peppers, sliced
½ cup zucchini, sliced
1 teaspoon olive oil
¼ teaspoon black pepper

⅛ teaspoon sea salt

INSTRUCTIONS

1. Preheat oven to 375°F (190°C). Toss the bell peppers, zucchini with one tsp oil, black pepper, and salt.
2. Roast the vegetables for 12–15 minutes until tender, then let cool slightly.
3. Spread hummus inside each pita half and fill with roasted veggies.
4. Serve warm as a nutritious and satisfying meal.

Nutritional Values (per serving): Calories: 290 | Total Carbs: 36g | Net Carbs: 30g | Sugar: 6g | Protein: 10g |

Fat: 12g | Saturated Fat: 2g | Cholesterol: 0mg | Sodium: 220mg

SPINACH & GRILLED CHICKEN STUFFED SWEET POTATO

 **PREP TIME:**
10 MINS

 COOK TIME:
45 MINS

 SERVING:
2

INGREDIENTS

2 medium sweet potatoes
1 boneless, skinless chicken breast
1 teaspoon olive oil
1 cup fresh spinach
¼ teaspoon black pepper

⅛ teaspoon sea salt

INSTRUCTIONS

1. Preheat oven to 400°F (200°C). Bake sweet potatoes for 40–45 minutes until fork-tender.
2. Massage the chicken with olive oil, black pepper, and salt, then grill for 6–7 minutes per side until cooked through.
3. Sauté the spinach in a dry skillet for 1 minute until wilted, then shred the grilled chicken and mix it in.
4. Slice open the baked sweet potatoes, stuff with the chicken-spinach mixture, and serve warm.

Nutritional Values (per serving):   Calories: 350 | Total Carbs: 45g | Net Carbs: 40g | Sugar: 8g | Protein: 28g |

Fat: 8g | Saturated Fat: 1g | Cholesterol: 75mg | Sodium: 210mg

BROWN RICE & GRILLED TOFU STIR-FRY

 PREP TIME: 10 MINS   **COOK TIME:** 60 MINS   **SERVING:** 2

INGREDIENTS

½ cup dry brown rice
1 cup firm tofu, cubed
½ cup broccoli florets
½ cup bell peppers, sliced
1 teaspoon olive oil
¼ teaspoon black pepper

⅛ teaspoon sea salt
½ cup dry brown rice
1 cup firm tofu, cubed
½ cup broccoli florets
½ cup bell peppers, sliced
1 teaspoon olive oil

¼ teaspoon black pepper
⅛ teaspoon sea salt

INSTRUCTIONS

1. Cook the brown rice in one cup water for 40 minutes, until tender, then set aside.
2. Heat a skillet, add olive oil, and grill tofu for 4–5 minutes, flipping until golden brown.
3. Toss in broccoli and bell peppers, and stir-fry for 3–4 minutes until tender.
4. Mix with the cooked brown rice, powder it with black pepper and salt, and serve warm.

Nutritional Values (per serving):   Calories: 320 | Total Carbs: 40g | Net Carbs: 34g | Sugar: 4g | Protein: 18g |
Fat: 10g | Saturated Fat: 1g | Cholesterol: 0mg | Sodium: 190mg

AVOCADO & TURKEY LETTUCE WRAPS

 PREP TIME: 5 MINS

 COOK TIME: 00 MINS

 SERVING: 2

INGREDIENTS

4 large romaine lettuce leaves
6 ounces turkey breast, sliced
½ avocado, sliced
¼ teaspoon black pepper

INSTRUCTIONS

1. Lay out the lettuce leaves on a plate.
2. Layer the turkey slices evenly across the leaves.
3. Top with avocado slices and sprinkle with black pepper.
4. Roll every leaf into a wrap and serve immediately.

Nutritional Values (per serving): Calories: 250 | Total Carbs: 8g | Net Carbs: 6g | Sugar: 2g | Protein: 26g |

Fat: 12g | Saturated Fat: 2g | Cholesterol: 55mg | Sodium: 210mg

LEMON HERB BAKED COD WITH ASPARAGUS

PREP TIME: 10 MINS	**COOK TIME:** 15 MINS	**SERVING:** 2

INGREDIENTS

2 cod fillets (4 oz each)
1 cup asparagus spears
1 teaspoon olive oil
1 teaspoon lemon juice
¼ teaspoon dried oregano
¼ teaspoon black pepper

⅛ teaspoon sea salt

INSTRUCTIONS

1. Preheat oven to 375°F (190°C). Arrange the baking sheet with parchment paper.
2. Place cod fillets and asparagus on the sheet, drizzle with olive oil and powder it with lemon juice, oregano, black pepper, and salt.
3. Bake for 12–15 minutes, until the cod is flaky and asparagus is tender.
4. Serve warm, garnished with extra lemon if desired.

Nutritional Values (per serving): Calories: 290 | Total Carbs: 6g | Net Carbs: 4g | Sugar: 1g | Protein: 36g |

Fat: 12g | Saturated Fat: 3g | Cholesterol: 85mg | Sodium: 220mg

WHOLE-WHEAT PASTA WITH ROASTED VEGETABLES & FETA

 PREP TIME:
10 MINS

 COOK TIME:
20 MINS

 SERVING:
2

INGREDIENTS

1 cup whole-wheat pasta
½ cup cherry tomatoes, halved
½ cup zucchini, diced
½ cup bell peppers, diced
1 teaspoon olive oil
¼ teaspoon black pepper

⅛ teaspoon sea salt
¼ cup crumbled feta cheese

INSTRUCTIONS

1. Preheat oven to 400°F (200°C). Toss the zucchini with bell peppers, and cherry tomatoes with one tsp oil, black pepper, and salt, and roast for 15 minutes.
2. Boil whole-wheat pasta in salted water for 8–10 minutes, then drain.
3. Combine pasta and roasted vegetables, toss well, and sprinkle with crumbled feta cheese.
4. Serve warm, garnished with extra black pepper if desired.

Nutritional Values (per serving): Calories: 350 | Total Carbs: 55g | Net Carbs: 48g | Sugar: 8g | Protein: 14g |

Fat: 10g | Saturated Fat: 3g | Cholesterol: 15mg | Sodium: 230mg

BALSAMIC GLAZED CHICKEN WITH ROASTED BRUSSELS SPROUTS

 PREP TIME: 10 MINS

 COOK TIME: 20 MINS

 SERVING: 2

INGREDIENTS

2 boneless, skinless chicken breasts
1 cup Brussels sprouts, halved
1 teaspoon olive oil
1 tablespoon balsamic vinegar
¼ teaspoon black pepper

⅛ teaspoon sea salt

INSTRUCTIONS

1. Preheat oven to 400°F (200°C). Massage the chicken with balsamic vinegar, black
2. pepper, and salt.
3. Toss Brussels sprouts with onet sp oil and place everything on the parchment paper-arranged baking sheet.
4. Roast for 18–20 minutes, flip after the halftime has passed, until the chicken is fully cooked and sprouts are caramelized.
5. Slice chicken and serve with the roasted Brussels sprouts.

Nutritional Values (per serving): Calories: 320 | Total Carbs: 12g | Net Carbs: 9g | Sugar: 3g | Protein: 36g |

Fat: 10g | Saturated Fat: 2g | Cholesterol: 85mg | Sodium: 210mg

STUFFED BELL PEPPERS WITH GROUND TURKEY & QUINOA

 PREP TIME: 10 MINS

 COOK TIME: 25 MINS

 SERVING: 2

INGREDIENTS

2 bell peppers, halved and deseeded
½ cup dry quinoa
½ pound ground turkey
½ cup diced tomatoes
1 teaspoon olive oil

¼ teaspoon black pepper
⅛ teaspoon sea salt

INSTRUCTIONS

1. Preheat oven to 375°F (190°C). Cook quinoa in one cup water for 15 minutes until fluffy.
2. Sauté ground turkey in olive oil for 5–6 minutes, then mix in quinoa, diced tomatoes, black pepper, and salt.
3. Stuff the bell pepper empty spaces with the mixture and bake for 20 minutes.
4. Serve warm, garnished with extra black pepper if desired.

Nutritional Values (per serving): Calories: 340 | Total Carbs: 30g | Net Carbs: 26g | Sugar: 6g | Protein: 32g |

Fat: 10g | Saturated Fat: 2g | Cholesterol: 75mg | Sodium: 220mg

GRILLED VEGGIE & HUMMUS WHOLE-WHEAT WRAP

 PREP TIME:
10 MINS

 COOK TIME:
10 MINS

 SERVING:
2

INGREDIENTS

2 whole-wheat tortillas
½ cup zucchini, sliced
½ cup bell peppers, sliced
½ cup mushrooms, sliced
1 teaspoon olive oil
¼ teaspoon black pepper

¼ cup hummus

INSTRUCTIONS

1. Heat a grill pan and grill the zucchini, bell peppers, and mushrooms with olive oil and black pepper for 5–6 minutes until tender.
2. Spread hummus evenly on the whole-wheat tortillas.
3. Layer the grilled vegetables, then roll tightly into wraps.
4. Slice in half and serve immediately.

Nutritional Values (per serving): Calories: 310 | Total Carbs: 42g | Net Carbs: 36g | Sugar: 7g | Protein: 10g |

Fat: 12g | Saturated Fat: 2g | Cholesterol: 0mg | Sodium: 200mg

SPICED LENTIL & ROASTED CAULIFLOWER BOWL

 PREP TIME:
10 MINS

 COOK TIME:
25 MINS

 SERVING:
2

INGREDIENTS

½ cup dry lentils
1 cup cauliflower florets
1 teaspoon olive oil
¼ teaspoon cumin
¼ teaspoon black pepper
⅛ teaspoon sea salt

INSTRUCTIONS

1. Preheat oven to 400°F (200°C). Toss cauliflower florets with olive oil, cumin, black pepper, and salt.
2. Roast cauliflower for 20 minutes until crispy, flipping halfway through.
3. Meanwhile, cook lentils in 1 cup of water for 15 minutes, then drain.
4. Combine lentils and roasted cauliflower, toss lightly, and serve warm.

Nutritional Values (per serving): Calories: 280 | Total Carbs: 38g | Net Carbs: 32g | Sugar: 5g | Protein: 14g |

Fat: 8g | Saturated Fat: 1g | Cholesterol: 0mg | Sodium: 180mg

ZUCCHINI NOODLES WITH PESTO & GRILLED CHICKEN

 PREP TIME:
10 MINS

 COOK TIME:
15 MINS

 SERVING:
2

INGREDIENTS

2 medium zucchinis, spiralized into noodles
2 boneless, skinless chicken breasts
1 teaspoon olive oil
¼ teaspoon black pepper

⅛ teaspoon sea salt
2 tablespoons pesto

INSTRUCTIONS

1. Preheat a grill pan. Massage the chicken with olive oil, black pepper, and salt. Grill for 6–7 minutes on one side until fully cooked, then slice.
2. Heat a skillet, add spiralized zucchini noodles, and sauté for 2 minutes until slightly softened.
3. Toss zucchini noodles with pesto, ensuring even coating.
4. Top with sliced grilled chicken and serve warm.

Nutritional Values (per serving): Calories: 320 | Total Carbs: 10g | Net Carbs: 7g | Sugar: 2g | Protein: 34g |

Fat: 14g | Saturated Fat: 3g | Cholesterol: 85mg | Sodium: 220mg

DINNER RECIPES

GRILLED CHICKEN WITH ROASTED SWEET POTATOES

 PREP TIME:
10 MINS

 COOK TIME:
30 MINS

 SERVING:
2

INGREDIENTS

2 boneless, skinless chicken breasts
1 medium sweet potato, diced
1 teaspoon olive oil
¼ teaspoon black pepper
⅛ teaspoon sea salt

½ teaspoon paprika

INSTRUCTIONS

1. Preheat oven to 400°F (200°C) and toss sweet potatoes with olive oil, paprika, black pepper, and salt, then roast for 25–30 minutes, flipping halfway.
2. Massage chicken with olive oil, black pepper, and salt, then grill for 6–7 minutes per side until fully cooked.
3. Remove chicken from heat, let it sit for 5 minutes, then slice.
4. Serve grilled chicken with roasted sweet potatoes on the side.

Nutritional Values (per serving): Calories: 350 | Total Carbs: 32g | Net Carbs: 28g | Sugar: 6g | Protein: 38g | Fat: 10g | Saturated Fat: 2g | Cholesterol: 85mg | Sodium: 220mg

STIR-FRIED TOFU WITH BROWN RICE & VEGETABLES

 PREP TIME:
10 MINS

 COOK TIME:
60 MINS

 SERVING:
2

INGREDIENTS

½ cup dry brown rice
1 cup firm tofu, cubed
½ cup bell peppers, sliced
½ cup broccoli florets
1 teaspoon olive oil
¼ teaspoon black pepper

⅛ teaspoon sea salt

INSTRUCTIONS

1. Cook brown rice in one cup water for 40 minutes until tender, then set aside.
2. Heat a skillet, add olive oil, and grill tofu for 4–5 minutes, flipping until golden.
3. Toss in bell peppers and broccoli, stir-fry for 3–4 minutes, then powder it with black pepper and salt.
4. Combine with cooked rice, mix well, and serve warm.

Nutritional Values (per serving): Calories: 320 | Total Carbs: 40g | Net Carbs: 34g | Sugar: 5g | Protein: 18g | Fat: 10g | Saturated Fat: 1g | Cholesterol: 0mg | Sodium: 190mg

BAKED COD WITH LEMON & GARLIC

 PREP TIME: 10 MINS

 COOK TIME: 15 MINS

 SERVING: 2

INGREDIENTS

2 cod fillets (4 oz each)
1 teaspoon olive oil
1 teaspoon lemon juice
1 teaspoon minced garlic
¼ teaspoon black pepper
⅛ teaspoon sea salt

INSTRUCTIONS

1. Preheat oven to 375°F (190°C). Arrange the baking sheet with parchment paper.
2. Place cod fillets on the sheet and rub with olive oil, lemon juice, garlic, black pepper, and salt.
3. Bake for 12–15 minutes, until flaky and fully cooked.
4. Serve immediately, garnished with extra lemon if desired.

Nutritional Values (per serving): Calories: 280 | Total Carbs: 2g | Net Carbs: 1g | Sugar: 0g | Protein: 36g |

Fat: 12g | Saturated Fat: 2g | Cholesterol: 85mg | Sodium: 200mg

TURKEY CHILI WITH BLACK BEANS & AVOCADO

 PREP TIME: 10 MINS   **COOK TIME:** 30 MINS   **SERVING:** 2

INGREDIENTS

½ pound ground turkey
½ cup dry black beans soaked overnight
½ cup diced tomatoes
½ cup diced bell peppers
½ teaspoon cumin

¼ teaspoon black pepper
1 teaspoon olive oil
½ avocado, sliced

INSTRUCTIONS

1. Drain and boil black beans in water for 20 minutes until tender, then drain.
2. Heat a pot, add olive oil, and cook ground turkey for 5 minutes, stirring to break it up.
3. Toss in black beans, tomatoes, bell peppers, cumin, and black pepper, then simmer for 15 minutes.
4. Serve hot, topped with sliced avocado.

Nutritional Values (per serving):   Calories: 360 | Total Carbs: 28g | Net Carbs: 24g | Sugar: 6g | Protein: 34g |

Fat: 14g | Saturated Fat: 3g | Cholesterol: 80mg | Sodium: 230mg

MEDITERRANEAN-STYLE STUFFED PEPPERS

 PREP TIME:
10 MINS

 COOK TIME:
30 MINS

 SERVING:
2

INGREDIENTS

2 bell peppers, halved and
deseeded
½ cup dry quinoa
½ pound ground turkey
½ cup diced tomatoes
1 teaspoon olive oil

¼ teaspoon black pepper
⅛ teaspoon sea salt

INSTRUCTIONS

1. Cook quinoa in one cup water for 15 minutes until fluffy.
2. Sauté ground turkey in olive oil for 5 minutes, then mix in quinoa, tomatoes, black pepper, and salt.
3. Stuff bell pepper halves with the mixture, then bake at 375°F (190°C) for 25 minutes.
4. Serve warm, optionally garnished with fresh parsley.

Nutritional Values (per serving): Calories: 340 | Total Carbs: 30g | Net Carbs: 26g | Sugar: 5g | Protein: 32g |

Fat: 10g | Saturated Fat: 2g | Cholesterol: 75mg | Sodium: 210mg

BALSAMIC GLAZED SALMON WITH STEAMED GREEN BEANS

 **PREP TIME:** 10 MINS   **COOK TIME:** 15 MINS   **SERVING:** 2

INGREDIENTS

2 salmon fillets (4 oz each)
1 teaspoon balsamic vinegar
1 teaspoon olive oil
1 cup green beans, trimmed
¼ teaspoon black pepper
⅛ teaspoon sea salt

INSTRUCTIONS

1. Preheat oven to 375°F (190°C). Massage the salmon fillets with balsamic vinegar, olive oil, black pepper, and salt.
2. Bake salmon for 12–15 minutes, until flaky.
3. Steam green beans in ½ inch of water for 3–4 minutes, then drain.
4. Serve salmon with steamed green beans on the side.

Nutritional Values (per serving):   Calories: 360 | Total Carbs: 6g | Net Carbs: 5g | Sugar: 2g | Protein: 34g |

Fat: 18g | Saturated Fat: 4g | Cholesterol: 85mg | Sodium: 220mg

QUINOA-STUFFED EGGPLANT WITH HERBS & PARMESAN

 PREP TIME:
10 MINS

 COOK TIME:
35 MINS

 SERVING:
2

INGREDIENTS

1 medium eggplant, halved and scooped
½ cup dry quinoa
½ cup diced tomatoes
¼ teaspoon black pepper
⅛ teaspoon sea salt

1 teaspoon olive oil
2 tablespoons grated Parmesan

INSTRUCTIONS

1. Preheat oven to 375°F (190°C). Roast eggplant halves for 15 minutes until slightly softened.
2. Cook quinoa in one cup water for 15 minutes, then mix in diced tomatoes, black pepper, salt, and olive oil.
3. Stuff eggplant halves with the quinoa mixture, then sprinkle with Parmesan and bake for 15 minutes.
4. Serve warm, spread fresh basil on top if desired.

Nutritional Values (per serving): Calories: 320 | Total Carbs: 42g | Net Carbs: 35g | Sugar: 7g | Protein: 14g |

Fat: 10g | Saturated Fat: 3g | Cholesterol: 10mg | Sodium: 200mg

LOW-SODIUM HERB ROASTED CHICKEN WITH QUINOA PILAF

 PREP TIME: 10 MINS

 COOK TIME: 35 MINS

 SERVING: 2

INGREDIENTS

2 boneless, skinless chicken breasts
½ teaspoon dried thyme
½ teaspoon dried rosemary
1 teaspoon olive oil
½ cup dry quinoa

½ cup diced bell peppers
¼ teaspoon black pepper
⅛ teaspoon sea salt

INSTRUCTIONS

1. Preheat oven to 375°F (190°C). Rub the chicken with thyme, rosemary, olive oil, black pepper, and salt.
2. Bake for 30–35 minutes, until fully cooked.
3. Cook quinoa in one cup water for 15 minutes, then stir in bell peppers and let sit for 5 minutes.
4. Serve roasted chicken over quinoa pilaf.

Nutritional Values (per serving): Calories: 350 | Total Carbs: 32g | Net Carbs: 28g | Sugar: 4g | Protein: 38g | Fat: 10g | Saturated Fat: 2g | Cholesterol: 85mg | Sodium: 210mg

GARLIC & LIME SHRIMP WITH WHOLE-WHEAT COUSCOUS

 PREP TIME: 10 MINS   **COOK TIME:** 15 MINS   **SERVING:** 2

INGREDIENTS

10 large shrimp, peeled and deveined
1 teaspoon olive oil
1 teaspoon lime juice
1 teaspoon minced garlic
½ cup dry whole-wheat couscous

¼ teaspoon black pepper
⅛ teaspoon sea salt

INSTRUCTIONS

1. Cook whole-wheat couscous by adding ½ cup boiling water, covering, and letting sit for 5 minutes, then fluff with a fork.
2. Toss shrimp with olive oil, lime juice, garlic, black pepper, and salt.
3. Sauté shrimp in a skillet on moderate heat for 2–3 minutes per side, until pink and opaque.
4. Serve shrimp over couscous, drizzling with extra lime juice if desired.

Nutritional Values (per serving): Calories: 320 | Total Carbs: 36g | Net Carbs: 32g | Sugar: 5g | Protein: 30g |

Fat: 8g | Saturated Fat: 1g | Cholesterol: 150mg | Sodium: 230mg

WHOLE-WHEAT PASTA WITH SPINACH, OLIVE OIL & GARLIC

 PREP TIME: 5 MINS

 COOK TIME: 12 MINS

 SERVING: 2

INGREDIENTS

1 cup whole-wheat pasta
1 cup fresh spinach
1 teaspoon olive oil
1 teaspoon minced garlic
¼ teaspoon black pepper
⅛ teaspoon sea salt

INSTRUCTIONS

1. Boil whole-wheat pasta in salted water for 8–10 minutes, then drain.
2. Heat one tsp oil in a skillet, then sauté garlic for 30 seconds until fragrant.
3. Toss in spinach and cook for 1–2 minutes, until wilted.
4. Mix pasta with spinach, powder it with black pepper and salt, and serve.

Nutritional Values (per serving): Calories: 340 | Total Carbs: 50g | Net Carbs: 45g | Sugar: 4g | Protein: 12g | Fat: 10g | Saturated Fat: 2g | Cholesterol: 0mg | Sodium: 220mg

LEAN BEEF STIR-FRY WITH BROWN RICE & PEPPERS

 PREP TIME:
10 MINS

 COOK TIME:
60 MINS

 SERVING:
2

INGREDIENTS

½ cup dry brown rice
6 oz lean beef, sliced
½ cup bell peppers, sliced
1 teaspoon olive oil
¼ teaspoon black pepper
⅛ teaspoon sea salt

INSTRUCTIONS

1. Cook brown rice in one cup water for 40 minutes, then set aside.
2. Heat a skillet, add olive oil, and sauté beef slices for 5 minutes, stirring occasionally.
3. Toss in bell peppers and stir-fry for 3–4 minutes, then powder it with black pepper and salt.
4. Serve stir-fry over cooked brown rice and enjoy warm.

Nutritional Values (per serving): Calories: 370 | Total Carbs: 40g | Net Carbs: 36g | Sugar: 6g | Protein: 32g |

Fat: 12g | Saturated Fat: 4g | Cholesterol: 80mg | Sodium: 230mg

GRILLED PORK TENDERLOIN WITH MASHED CAULIFLOWER

 **PREP TIME:**
10 MINS

 COOK TIME:
25 MINS

 SERVING:
2

INGREDIENTS

6 oz pork tenderloin
1 teaspoon olive oil
½ teaspoon dried rosemary
1 cup cauliflower florets
¼ teaspoon black pepper
⅛ teaspoon sea salt

INSTRUCTIONS

1. Preheat oven to 375°F (190°C). Massage the pork with olive oil, rosemary, black pepper, and salt.
2. Grill pork for 6–7 minutes per side, then let rest for 5 minutes before slicing.
3. Steam cauliflower for 5 minutes, then mash with a fork and season.
4. Serve grilled pork over mashed cauliflower.

Nutritional Values (per serving): Calories: 320 | Total Carbs: 8g | Net Carbs: 6g | Sugar: 2g | Protein: 36g |

Fat: 12g | Saturated Fat: 3g | Cholesterol: 85mg | Sodium: 200mg

SWEET POTATO & BLACK BEAN ENCHILADAS (LOW-SODIUM)

 PREP TIME: 10 MINS

 COOK TIME: 25 MINS

 SERVING: 2

INGREDIENTS

2 small whole-wheat tortillas
1 small sweet potato, diced
½ cup dry black beans soaked overnight
½ teaspoon cumin
¼ teaspoon black pepper

1 teaspoon olive oil

INSTRUCTIONS

1. Boil sweet potatoes until fork-tender, about 8 minutes, then drain.
2. Drain and cook black beans in water for 20 minutes, then mash slightly.
3. Mix black beans with sweet potatoes, cumin, black pepper, and olive oil, then fill the tortillas and roll.
4. Bake at 375°F (190°C) for 15 minutes and serve warm.

Nutritional Values (per serving): Calories: 340 | Total Carbs: 50g | Net Carbs: 44g | Sugar: 6g | Protein: 14g |

Fat: 8g | Saturated Fat: 1g | Cholesterol: 0mg | Sodium: 210mg

ROASTED CHICKEN WITH ROASTED VEGETABLES

 **PREP TIME:**
10 MINS

 COOK TIME:
40 MINS

 SERVING:
2

INGREDIENTS

2 bone-in chicken thighs
1 teaspoon olive oil
½ teaspoon dried thyme
1 cup carrots, sliced
1 cup zucchini, diced
¼ teaspoon black pepper

⅛ teaspoon sea salt

INSTRUCTIONS

1. Preheat oven to 400°F (200°C). Rub chicken thighs with olive oil, thyme, black pepper, and salt.
2. Roast chicken for 35–40 minutes, until crispy and fully cooked.
3. Toss carrots and zucchini with olive oil, then roast for 20 minutes, stirring halfway.
4. Serve roasted chicken with roasted vegetables on the side.

Nutritional Values (per serving): Calories: 390 | Total Carbs: 20g | Net Carbs: 16g | Sugar: 5g | Protein: 38g |

Fat: 18g | Saturated Fat: 5g | Cholesterol: 95mg | Sodium: 230mg

TOFU & BROCCOLI STIR-FRY WITH CASHEWS

 PREP TIME: 10 MINS   **COOK TIME:** 15 MINS   **SERVING:** 2

INGREDIENTS

1 cup firm tofu, cubed
1 cup broccoli florets
¼ cup raw cashews
1 teaspoon olive oil
1 teaspoon low-sodium soy sauce
¼ teaspoon black pepper

INSTRUCTIONS

1. Heat one tsp oil in a skillet and sauté tofu for 5 minutes, flipping until golden.
2. Add broccoli and cashews, stir-frying for 3–4 minutes until slightly tender.
3. Drizzle with soy sauce and black pepper, stirring to coat evenly.
4. Serve warm as a protein-packed, nutrient-dense meal.

Nutritional Values (per serving):   Calories: 320 | Total Carbs: 32g | Net Carbs: 26g | Sugar: 5g | Protein: 18g |

Fat: 14g | Saturated Fat: 2g | Cholesterol: 0mg | Sodium: 200mg

GRILLED SALMON WITH MANGO SALSA & BROWN RICE

| PREP TIME: 10 MINS | COOK TIME: 60 MINS | SERVING: 2 |

INGREDIENTS

2 salmon fillets (4 oz each)
1 teaspoon olive oil
½ teaspoon cumin
½ cup dry brown rice
½ cup diced mango
¼ cup diced red onion

1 teaspoon lime juice
¼ teaspoon black pepper

INSTRUCTIONS

1. Cook brown rice in one cup water for 40 minutes, then set aside.
2. Massage salmon with olive oil, cumin, and black pepper, then grill for 6–7 minutes per side until flaky.
3. Mix mango, red onion, lime juice, and black pepper to create the salsa.
4. Serve grilled salmon over brown rice, topped with mango salsa.

Nutritional Values (per serving): Calories: 380 | Total Carbs: 36g | Net Carbs: 32g | Sugar: 7g | Protein: 36g |

Fat: 14g | Saturated Fat: 3g | Cholesterol: 85mg | Sodium: 220mg

TURKEY MEATBALLS WITH WHOLE-WHEAT SPAGHETTI

 PREP TIME:
10 MINS

 COOK TIME:
25 MINS

 SERVING:
2

INGREDIENTS

½ pound ground turkey
½ teaspoon oregano
¼ teaspoon black pepper
½ teaspoon minced garlic
1 teaspoon olive oil
1 cup whole-wheat spaghetti

½ cup crushed tomatoes

INSTRUCTIONS

1. Mix turkey with oregano, black pepper, and garlic, then form into meatballs.
2. Heat one tsp oil in a pan, add meatballs, and cook for 8–10 minutes, turning occasionally.
3. Boil whole-wheat spaghetti in salted water for 10 minutes, then drain.
4. Simmer crushed tomatoes for 5 minutes, then toss with spaghetti and meatballs before serving.

Nutritional Values (per serving): Calories: 400 | Total Carbs: 45g | Net Carbs: 40g | Sugar: 6g | Protein: 38g |

Fat: 12g | Saturated Fat: 3g | Cholesterol: 90mg | Sodium: 240mg

STUFFED ACORN SQUASH WITH WILD RICE & NUTS

 PREP TIME: 10 MINS   **COOK TIME:** 45 MINS   **SERVING:** 2

INGREDIENTS

1 medium acorn squash, halved and seeded
½ cup dry wild rice
¼ cup chopped walnuts
1 teaspoon olive oil
¼ teaspoon black pepper

⅛ teaspoon sea salt

INSTRUCTIONS

1. Preheat oven to 375°F (190°C). Roast acorn squash halves for 30 minutes until soft.
2. Cook wild rice in one cup water for 20 minutes, then mix with walnuts, olive oil, black pepper, and salt.
3. Stuff the roasted squash halves with the wild rice mixture.
4. Return to oven for 10 minutes, then serve warm.

Nutritional Values (per serving): Calories: 350 | Total Carbs: 50g | Net Carbs: 44g | Sugar: 8g | Protein: 10g |
Fat: 14g | Saturated Fat: 2g | Cholesterol: 0mg | Sodium: 200mg

ROASTED BRUSSELS SPROUTS & QUINOA WITH ALMONDS

 PREP TIME: 10 MINS   **COOK TIME:** 25 MINS   **SERVING:** 2

INGREDIENTS

1 cup Brussels sprouts, halved
½ cup dry quinoa
¼ cup sliced almonds
1 teaspoon olive oil
¼ teaspoon black pepper
⅛ teaspoon sea salt

INSTRUCTIONS

1. Preheat oven to 400°F (200°C). Toss the Brussels sprouts with one tsp oil, black pepper, and salt, then roast for 20 minutes.
2. Cook quinoa in 1 cup of water for 15 minutes, then let sit for 5 minutes.
3. Toast sliced almonds in a dry pan for 1–2 minutes until fragrant.
4. Mix roasted Brussels sprouts with quinoa and almonds, then serve warm.

Nutritional Values (per serving): Calories: 320 | Total Carbs: 40g | Net Carbs: 34g | Sugar: 6g | Protein: 14g |

Fat: 10g | Saturated Fat: 1g | Cholesterol: 0mg | Sodium: 190mg

BAKED TILAPIA WITH GARLIC & ROASTED CARROTS

 PREP TIME: 10 MINS

 COOK TIME: 20 MINS

 SERVING: 2

INGREDIENTS

2 tilapia fillets (4 oz each)
1 teaspoon olive oil
1 teaspoon minced garlic
1 cup baby carrots
¼ teaspoon black pepper
⅛ teaspoon sea salt

INSTRUCTIONS

1. Preheat oven to 375°F (190°C), then rub tilapia with olive oil, garlic, black pepper, and salt.
2. Place the tilapia and carrots on the parchment paper-arranged baking sheet, then bake for 15–20 minutes until the tilapia is flaky and the carrots are tender.
3. Toss roasted carrots with an extra drizzle of olive oil for flavor.
4. Serve baked tilapia with roasted carrots on the side.

Nutritional Values (per serving): Calories: 310 | Total Carbs: 12g | Net Carbs: 10g | Sugar: 5g | Protein: 34g |

Fat: 12g | Saturated Fat: 2g | Cholesterol: 85mg | Sodium: 210mg

SOUPS & STEWS

HEARTY VEGETABLE SOUP WITH LENTILS

 **PREP TIME:**
10 MINS

 COOK TIME:
30 MINS

 SERVING:
2

INGREDIENTS

½ cup dry lentils
1 cup diced carrots
½ cup diced celery
½ cup diced zucchini
2 cups low-sodium vegetable broth

1 teaspoon olive oil
½ teaspoon dried oregano
¼ teaspoon black pepper

INSTRUCTIONS

1. Heat one tsp oil in a large pot, then sauté carrots, celery, and zucchini for 5 minutes until slightly tender.
2. Rinse lentils and add them to the shallow pot with vegetable broth, oregano, and black pepper.
3. Get it to a boil, then decrease the stove heat and simmer for 25 minutes, stirring occasionally.
4. Serve warm, optionally garnished with fresh parsley.

Nutritional Values (per serving): Calories: 310 | Total Carbs: 48g | Net Carbs: 36g | Sugar: 10g | Protein: 16g | Fat: 6g | Saturated Fat: 1g | Cholesterol: 0mg | Sodium: 180mg

LOW-SODIUM MINESTRONE WITH WHOLE-GRAIN PASTA

PREP TIME: 10 MINS

COOK TIME: 25 MINS

SERVING: 2

INGREDIENTS

½ cup whole-grain pasta
½ cup kidney beans soaked overnight
½ cup diced tomatoes
½ cup diced carrots
½ cup chopped spinach

2 cups low-sodium vegetable broth
1 teaspoon olive oil
½ teaspoon dried basil

INSTRUCTIONS

1. Boil kidney beans in water for 15 minutes, then drain and set aside.
2. Heat one tsp oil in a pot, then sauté carrots and tomatoes for 5 minutes until softened.
3. Add kidney beans, pasta, vegetable broth, and basil, then simmer for 15 minutes until pasta is tender.
4. Stir in spinach, cook for 2 more minutes, then serve warm.

Nutritional Values (per serving): Calories: 340 | Total Carbs: 52g | Net Carbs: 40g | Sugar: 8g | Protein: 18g | Fat: 8g | Saturated Fat: 1g | Cholesterol: 0mg | Sodium: 190mg

TOMATO BASIL SOUP WITH QUINOA

 PREP TIME:
10 MINS

 COOK TIME:
20 MINS

 SERVING:
2

INGREDIENTS

1 cup diced tomatoes
½ cup dry quinoa
2 cups low-sodium vegetable broth
1 teaspoon olive oil
½ teaspoon dried basil

¼ teaspoon black pepper
1 teaspoon minced garlic

INSTRUCTIONS

1. Heat one tsp oil in a pot, then sauté garlic and diced tomatoes for 3–4 minutes until softened.
2. Rinse quinoa and add it to the shallow pot with vegetable broth, basil, and black pepper.
3. Get it to a boil, then decrease the stove heat and simmer for 15 minutes, stirring occasionally.
4. Serve warm, optionally garnished with fresh basil leaves.

Nutritional Values (per serving): Calories: 300 | Total Carbs: 46g | Net Carbs: 36g | Sugar: 9g | Protein: 12g |
Fat: 6g | Saturated Fat: 1g | Cholesterol: 0mg | Sodium: 170mg

LENTIL & KALE STEW WITH GARLIC & HERBS

 PREP TIME:
10 MINS

 COOK TIME:
30 MINS

 SERVING:
2

INGREDIENTS

½ cup dry lentils
1 cup chopped kale
½ cup diced carrots
½ teaspoon dried thyme
1 teaspoon minced garlic
2 cups low-sodium vegetable

broth
1 teaspoon olive oil
¼ teaspoon black pepper

INSTRUCTIONS

1. Heat one tsp oil in a pot, then sauté garlic and carrots for 5 minutes until fragrant.
2. Rinse lentils and add them to the shallow pot with vegetable broth, thyme, and black pepper.
3. Get it to a boil, then decrease the stove heat and simmer for 25 minutes, stirring occasionally.
4. Stir in chopped kale, cook for 2 more minutes, then serve warm.

Nutritional Values (per serving): Calories: 320 | Total Carbs: 45g | Net Carbs: 33g | Sugar: 7g | Protein: 18g |

Fat: 8g | Saturated Fat: 1g | Cholesterol: 0mg | Sodium: 180mg

CHICKEN & BROWN RICE SOUP (LOW-SODIUM)

 **PREP TIME:**
10 MINS

 COOK TIME:
70 MINS

 SERVING:
2

INGREDIENTS

½ cup dry brown rice
1 boneless, skinless chicken breast
½ cup diced celery
½ cup diced carrots
2 cups low-sodium chicken broth

1 teaspoon olive oil
½ teaspoon dried oregano
¼ teaspoon black pepper

INSTRUCTIONS

1. Cook brown rice in one cup water for 40 minutes, then set aside.
2. Heat one tsp oil in a pot, then sauté chicken, carrots, and celery for 5 minutes.
3. Add chicken broth, oregano, and black pepper, then simmer for 20 minutes until the chicken is fully cooked.
4. Shred the chicken, stir in the brown rice, and serve warm.

Nutritional Values (per serving): Calories: 350 | Total Carbs: 32g | Net Carbs: 26g | Sugar: 4g | Protein: 36g |
Fat: 10g | Saturated Fat: 2g | Cholesterol: 70mg | Sodium: 200mg

SPICED SWEET POTATO & CARROT SOUP

 PREP TIME:
10 MINS

 COOK TIME:
25 MINS

 SERVING:
2

INGREDIENTS

1 medium sweet potato, peeled and diced
1 cup carrots, chopped
2 cups low-sodium vegetable broth
1 teaspoon olive oil

½ teaspoon ground cumin
¼ teaspoon cinnamon
¼ teaspoon black pepper

INSTRUCTIONS

1. Heat one tsp oil in a pot, then sauté carrots and sweet potato for 5 minutes until slightly softened.
2. Add vegetable broth, cumin, cinnamon, and black pepper, then get it to a boil.
3. Decrease the stove heat and simmer for 20 minutes, until vegetables are tender, then blend until smooth.
4. Serve warm, optionally garnished with fresh herbs.

Nutritional Values (per serving): Calories: 310 | Total Carbs: 58g | Net Carbs: 48g | Sugar: 12g | Protein: 6g |

Fat: 6g | Saturated Fat: 1g | Cholesterol: 0mg | Sodium: 180mg

MEDITERRANEAN CHICKPEA & SPINACH STEW

 PREP TIME:
10 MINS

 COOK TIME:
25 MINS

 SERVING:
2

INGREDIENTS

½ cup dry chickpeas, soaked overnight
1 cup fresh spinach
½ cup diced tomatoes
2 cups low-sodium vegetable broth

1 teaspoon olive oil
½ teaspoon dried oregano
¼ teaspoon black pepper

INSTRUCTIONS

1. Drain and cook chickpeas in water for 15–20 minutes until tender, then set aside.
2. Heat one tsp oil in a pot, then sauté tomatoes with oregano and black pepper for 5 minutes.
3. Add chickpeas and vegetable broth, then simmer for 15 minutes.
4. Stir in spinach, cook for 2 minutes, then serve warm.

Nutritional Values (per serving): Calories: 340 | Total Carbs: 48g | Net Carbs: 36g | Sugar: 10g | Protein: 18g | Fat: 8g | Saturated Fat: 1g | Cholesterol: 0mg | Sodium: 190mg

ROASTED RED PEPPER & TOMATO SOUP

 PREP TIME:
10 MINS

 COOK TIME:
25 MINS

 SERVING:
2

INGREDIENTS

2 large red bell peppers, halved and deseeded
1 cup diced tomatoes
2 cups low-sodium vegetable broth
1 teaspoon olive oil

½ teaspoon dried basil
¼ teaspoon black pepper

INSTRUCTIONS

1. Preheat oven to 400°F (200°C). Roast bell peppers for 20 minutes until charred, then peel and chop.
2. Heat one tsp oil in a pot, then sauté diced tomatoes with basil and black pepper for 5 minutes.
3. Add roasted peppers and vegetable broth, then simmer for 10 minutes.
4. Blend until smooth, then serve warm.

Nutritional Values (per serving): Calories: 290 | Total Carbs: 40g | Net Carbs: 30g | Sugar: 8g | Protein: 10g | Fat: 8g | Saturated Fat: 1g | Cholesterol: 0mg | Sodium: 180mg

QUINOA & BLACK BEAN CHILI SOUP

 **PREP TIME:**
10 MINS

 COOK TIME:
30 MINS

 SERVING:
2

INGREDIENTS

½ cup dry quinoa
½ cup dry black beans soaked overnight
½ cup diced bell peppers
½ cup diced tomatoes
2 cups low-sodium vegetable broth
1 teaspoon olive oil
½ teaspoon chili powder

INSTRUCTIONS

1. Cook black beans in water for 20 minutes until tender, then drain.
2. Heat one tsp oil in a pot, then sauté bell peppers and tomatoes for 5 minutes.
3. Add quinoa, black beans, vegetable broth, and chili powder, then simmer for 20 minutes.
4. Serve warm, optionally garnished with fresh cilantro.

Nutritional Values (per serving):   Calories: 350 | Total Carbs: 50g | Net Carbs: 38g | Sugar: 9g | Protein: 18g | Fat: 8g | Saturated Fat: 1g | Cholesterol: 0mg | Sodium: 190mg

COCONUT CURRY LENTIL SOUP

 PREP TIME:
10 MINS

 COOK TIME:
30 MINS

 SERVING:
2

INGREDIENTS

½ cup dry lentils
1 cup diced carrots
2 cups low-sodium vegetable broth
½ cup light coconut milk
1 teaspoon olive oil

½ teaspoon curry powder
¼ teaspoon black pepper

INSTRUCTIONS

1. Heat one tsp oil in a pot, then sauté carrots and curry powder for 5 minutes.
2. Rinse lentils and add them to the deep-bottom pot with vegetable broth and black pepper.
3. Simmer for 25 minutes, until the lentils gets tenderness, then stir in coconut milk.
4. Serve warm, optionally garnished with fresh cilantro.

Nutritional Values (per serving): Calories: 330 | Total Carbs: 50g | Net Carbs: 38g | Sugar: 11g | Protein: 14g | Fat: 10g | Saturated Fat: 3g | Cholesterol: 0mg | Sodium: 200mg

SNACKS & SIDES

HUMMUS WITH CARROT & CUCUMBER STICKS

 PREP TIME: 10 MINS

 COOK TIME: 00 MINS

 SERVING: 2

INGREDIENTS

½ cup cooked chickpeas
1 teaspoon olive oil
½ teaspoon lemon juice
½ teaspoon minced garlic
¼ teaspoon black pepper
1 small carrot, cut into sticks

1 small cucumber, cut into sticks

INSTRUCTIONS

1. Blend chickpeas, olive oil, lemon juice, garlic, and black pepper in a food blender until smooth.
2. Adjust consistency by adding a teaspoon of water if needed.
3. Arrange carrot and cucumber sticks on a serving plate.
4. Serve hummus with vegetable sticks as a dip.

Nutritional Values (per serving): Calories: 220 | Total Carbs: 28g | Net Carbs: 22g | Sugar: 5g | Protein: 8g |

Fat: 10g | Saturated Fat: 1g | Cholesterol: 0mg | Sodium: 150mg

HANDFUL OF UNSALTED ALMONDS & WALNUTS

 **PREP TIME:**
10 MINS

 COOK TIME:
00 MINS

 SERVING:
2

INGREDIENTS

¼ cup raw almonds
¼ cup raw walnuts

INSTRUCTIONS

1. Measure almonds and walnuts into a small bowl.
2. Check for freshness, ensuring the nuts are not stale.
3. Divide into portions, keeping them in small containers for easy snacking.
4. Enjoy as is, or lightly toast if desired for extra crunch.

Nutritional Values (per serving): Calories: 240 | Total Carbs: 8g | Net Carbs: 4g | Sugar: 2g | Protein: 7g | Fat: 22g | Saturated Fat: 2g | Cholesterol: 0mg | Sodium: 0mg

APPLE SLICES WITH PEANUT BUTTER

 PREP TIME:
5 MINS

 COOK TIME:
00 MINS

 SERVING:
2

INGREDIENTS

1 medium apple, sliced
2 tablespoons natural peanut butter

INSTRUCTIONS

1. Wash and slice the apple into even wedges.
2. Spoon peanut butter into a small dish.
3. Dip every apple slice into the peanut butter or spread it on top.
4. Serve immediately as a balanced and satisfying snack.

Nutritional Values (per serving): Calories: 250 | Total Carbs: 28g | Net Carbs: 22g | Sugar: 18g | Protein: 8g |
Fat: 14g | Saturated Fat: 2g | Cholesterol: 0mg | Sodium: 120mg

LOW-FAT COTTAGE CHEESE WITH BLUEBERRIES

 PREP TIME: 5 MINS

 COOK TIME: 00 MINS

 SERVING: 2

INGREDIENTS

1 cup low-fat cottage cheese
½ cup fresh blueberries

INSTRUCTIONS

1. Scoop cottage cheese into a serving bowl.
2. Wash and pat dry blueberries, then sprinkle over the top.
3. Gently mix if desired for an even blend.
4. Serve fresh, optionally adding a drizzle of honey for extra sweetness.

Nutritional Values (per serving): Calories: 180 | Total Carbs: 20g | Net Carbs: 18g | Sugar: 10g | Protein: 18g
| Fat: 4g | Saturated Fat: 1g | Cholesterol: 10mg | Sodium: 180mg

ROASTED CHICKPEAS WITH SMOKED PAPRIKA

 PREP TIME:
10 MINS

 COOK TIME:
30 MINS

 SERVING:
2

INGREDIENTS

½ cup dry chickpeas, soaked
overnight
1 teaspoon olive oil
½ teaspoon smoked paprika
¼ teaspoon black pepper
⅛ teaspoon sea salt

INSTRUCTIONS

1. Boil chickpeas for 15–20 minutes until tender, then drain and pat dry.
2. Preheat oven to 375°F (190°C). Toss the chickpeas with olive oil, paprika, black pepper, and salt.
3. Spread on the parchment paper-arranged baking sheet and roast for 25–30 minutes, shaking halfway.
4. Let cool slightly, then serve crunchy as a snack.

Nutritional Values (per serving): Calories: 230 | Total Carbs: 32g | Net Carbs: 26g | Sugar: 3g | Protein: 10g |

Fat: 8g | Saturated Fat: 1g | Cholesterol: 0mg | Sodium: 170mg

BAKED SWEET POTATO FRIES WITH GARLIC & HERBS

 **PREP TIME:**
10 MINS

 COOK TIME:
25 MINS

 SERVING:
2

INGREDIENTS

1 medium sweet potato, cut into fries
1 teaspoon olive oil
½ teaspoon minced garlic
¼ teaspoon dried rosemary
¼ teaspoon black pepper

INSTRUCTIONS

1. Preheat oven to 400°F (200°C). Arrange the baking sheet with parchment paper.
2. Toss sweet potato fries with one tsp oil, garlic, rosemary, and black pepper.
3. Spread in a single layer and bake for 20–25 minutes, flipping halfway.
4. Serve warm, optionally, with a yogurt-based dip.

Nutritional Values (per serving): Calories: 230 | Total Carbs: 40g | Net Carbs: 34g | Sugar: 9g | Protein: 4g |

Fat: 7g | Saturated Fat: 1g | Cholesterol: 0mg | Sodium: 160mg

WHOLE-WHEAT CRACKERS WITH AVOCADO & FETA

 PREP TIME: 5 MINS

 COOK TIME: 00 MINS

 SERVING: 2

INGREDIENTS

8 whole-wheat crackers
½ avocado, mashed
2 tablespoons crumbled feta cheese
¼ teaspoon black pepper

INSTRUCTIONS

1. Mash avocado in a small deep-bottom bowl and mix in black pepper.
2. Spread mashed avocado evenly on each cracker.
3. Sprinkle crumbled feta on top for extra flavor.
4. Serve immediately as a crunchy and creamy snack.

Nutritional Values (per serving): Calories: 250 | Total Carbs: 30g | Net Carbs: 24g | Sugar: 2g | Protein: 6g |

Fat: 12g | Saturated Fat: 3g | Cholesterol: 5mg | Sodium: 180mg

GREEK YOGURT WITH CINNAMON & FLAXSEEDS

 PREP TIME:
5 MINS

 COOK TIME:
00 MINS

 SERVING:
2

INGREDIENTS

1 cup Greek yogurt (low-fat)
½ teaspoon ground cinnamon
1 tablespoon ground flaxseeds

INSTRUCTIONS

1. Scoop Greek yogurt into a serving bowl.
2. Sprinkle cinnamon and flaxseeds evenly over the top.
3. Gently mix to combine flavors.
4. Serve fresh, optionally, with a drizzle of honey.

Nutritional Values (per serving): Calories: 180 | Total Carbs: 22g | Net Carbs: 18g | Sugar: 6g | Protein: 6g |

Fat: 8g | Saturated Fat: 1g | Cholesterol: 0mg | Sodium: 140mg

CUCUMBER SLICES WITH HUMMUS & CHERRY TOMATOES

 PREP TIME:
5 MINS

 COOK TIME:
00 MINS

 SERVING:
2

INGREDIENTS

1 small cucumber, sliced
¼ cup hummus
6 cherry tomatoes, halved

INSTRUCTIONS

1. Arrange cucumber slices on a serving plate.
2. Dollop hummus onto each slice for flavor.
3. Top with halved cherry tomatoes for a fresh crunch.
4. Serve immediately as a light and refreshing snack.

Nutritional Values (per serving): Calories: 180 | Total Carbs: 22g | Net Carbs: 18g | Sugar: 6g | Protein: 6g |

Fat: 8g | Saturated Fat: 1g | Cholesterol: 0mg | Sodium: 140mg

HARD-BOILED EGGS WITH WHOLE-GRAIN CRACKERS

	PREP TIME: 5 MINS		COOK TIME: 10 MINS		SERVING: 2

INGREDIENTS

4 large eggs
8 whole-grain crackers
¼ teaspoon black pepper
⅛ teaspoon sea salt

INSTRUCTIONS

1. Place eggs in a saucepan, cover with water, and get it to a boil on moderate heat.
2. Once boiling, decrease the stove heat and cook for 8–10 minutes, then transfer to ice water for 5 minutes.
3. Peel eggs, slice them in half, and powder them with salt and black pepper.
4. Serve immediately with whole-grain crackers.

Nutritional Values (per serving): Calories: 220 | Total Carbs: 18g | Net Carbs: 14g | Sugar: 2g | Protein: 16g | Fat: 10g | Saturated Fat: 3g | Cholesterol: 190mg | Sodium: 210mg

SMOOTHIES & DRINKS

GREEN SMOOTHIE WITH SPINACH, BANANA & ALMOND MILK

 PREP TIME: 5 MINS

 COOK TIME: 00 MINS

 SERVING: 2

INGREDIENTS

1 cup fresh spinach
1 medium banana
1 cup unsweetened almond milk
½ teaspoon ground flaxseeds
3–4 ice cubes

INSTRUCTIONS

1. Rinse spinach and peel banana, then add both to a blender.
2. Ladle almond milk and add flaxseeds for extra fiber.
3. Blend until smooth, adding ice cubes for a chilled texture.
4. Serve immediately, optionally garnished with a spinach leaf.

Nutritional Values (per serving): Calories: 180 | Total Carbs: 30g | Net Carbs: 25g | Sugar: 15g | Protein: 6g |

Fat: 5g | Saturated Fat: 1g | Cholesterol: 0mg | Sodium: 140mg

BERRY & CHIA PROTEIN SMOOTHIE

 PREP TIME:
5 MINS

 COOK TIME:
00 MINS

 SERVING:
2

INGREDIENTS

½ cup mixed berries
(strawberries, blueberries,
raspberries)
1 tablespoon chia seeds
1 cup unsweetened almond milk
½ scoop plant-based protein

powder
3–4 ice cubes

INSTRUCTIONS

1. Wash berries and add them to a blender with chia seeds.
2. Ladle almond milk and add protein powder for an extra boost.
3. Blend until smooth, adding ice cubes for a thicker consistency.
4. Serve fresh, optionally topped with extra chia seeds.

Nutritional Values (per serving): Calories: 210 | Total Carbs: 28g | Net Carbs: 24g | Sugar: 14g | Protein: 12g
| Fat: 7g | Saturated Fat: 1g | Cholesterol: 0mg | Sodium: 120mg

LOW-SODIUM TOMATO JUICE BLEND

 PREP TIME:
5 MINS

 COOK TIME:
00 MINS

 SERVING:
2

INGREDIENTS

2 large tomatoes, chopped
½ cup celery, chopped
½ teaspoon lemon juice
¼ teaspoon black pepper
½ cup cold water

INSTRUCTIONS

1. Add chopped tomatoes and celery to a blender.
2. Ladle water and lemon juice, then blend until smooth.
3. Strain through a sieve if a smoother texture is preferred.
4. Serve immediately, seasoned with black pepper.

Nutritional Values (per serving): Calories: 80 | Total Carbs: 18g | Net Carbs: 15g | Sugar: 10g | Protein: 3g |

Fat: 1g | Saturated Fat: 0g | Cholesterol: 0mg | Sodium: 75mg

CUCUMBER & MINT HYDRATION DRINK

 PREP TIME: 5 MINS

 COOK TIME: 00 MINS

 SERVING: 2

INGREDIENTS

1 small cucumber, sliced
4 fresh mint leaves
2 cups cold water
½ teaspoon lemon juice

INSTRUCTIONS

1. Wash and slice cucumber, then add to a pitcher with mint leaves.
2. Ladle cold water and add lemon juice for a refreshing taste.
3. Let it sit for 5 minutes to infuse the flavors.
4. Serve chilled, optionally, with ice cubes.

Nutritional Values (per serving): Calories: 20 | Total Carbs: 4g | Net Carbs: 3g | Sugar: 1g | Protein: 1g | Fat: 0g | Saturated Fat: 0g | Cholesterol: 0mg | Sodium: 20mg

ALMOND BUTTER & BANANA SMOOTHIE

 **PREP TIME:** 5 MINS   **COOK TIME:** 00 MINS   **SERVING:** 2

INGREDIENTS

1 medium banana
1 tablespoon almond butter
1 cup unsweetened almond milk
½ teaspoon ground cinnamon
3–4 ice cubes

INSTRUCTIONS

1. Peel the banana and add to a blender with almond butter.
2. Ladle almond milk and add cinnamon for a warm flavor.
3. Blend until smooth, adding ice cubes for thickness.
4. Serve immediately, optionally topped with extra cinnamon.

Nutritional Values (per serving): Calories: 250 | Total Carbs: 36g | Net Carbs: 30g | Sugar: 18g | Protein: 7g | Fat: 10g | Saturated Fat: 1g | Cholesterol: 0mg | Sodium: 140mg

STRAWBERRY & FLAXSEED YOGURT SMOOTHIE

 PREP TIME: 5 MINS

 COOK TIME: 00 MINS

 SERVING: 2

INGREDIENTS

½ cup fresh strawberries, hulled
1 cup low-fat Greek yogurt
1 tablespoon ground flaxseeds
½ teaspoon vanilla extract
3–4 ice cubes

INSTRUCTIONS

1. Wash and hull strawberries, then add them to a blender.
2. Add Greek yogurt, flaxseeds, and vanilla extract for added creaminess and fiber.
3. Blend until smooth, adding ice cubes for a chilled texture.
4. Serve immediately, optionally garnished with a strawberry slice.

Nutritional Values (per serving): Calories: 200 | Total Carbs: 24g | Net Carbs: 20g | Sugar: 12g | Protein: 14g | Fat: 5g | Saturated Fat: 2g | Cholesterol: 10mg | Sodium: 160mg

WATERMELON & COCONUT WATER REFRESHER

	PREP TIME: 5 MINS		COOK TIME: 00 MINS		SERVING: 2

INGREDIENTS

1 cup fresh watermelon, cubed
1 cup coconut water
½ teaspoon lime juice
3–4 ice cubes

INSTRUCTIONS

1. Add watermelon cubes to a blender, then Ladle coconut water.
2. Blend until smooth, adding lime juice for a refreshing tang.
3. Strain if desired, then Ladleto glasses over ice.
4. Serve immediately, optionally garnished with a lime wedge.

Nutritional Values (per serving): Calories: 90 | Total Carbs: 22g | Net Carbs: 20g | Sugar: 18g | Protein: 1g |

Fat: 0g | Saturated Fat: 0g | Cholesterol: 0mg | Sodium: 35mg

LOW-SUGAR ALMOND MILK LATTE

 PREP TIME: 5 MINS

 COOK TIME: 5 MINS

 SERVING: 2

INGREDIENTS

1 cup brewed coffee
1 cup unsweetened almond milk
½ teaspoon vanilla extract
¼ teaspoon ground cinnamon

INSTRUCTIONS

1. Brew fresh coffee and set it aside.
2. Heat almond milk in a saucepan on moderate heat until warm, then whisk until frothy.
3. Pour hot coffee into a mug, then add the frothed almond milk.
4. Sprinkle with cinnamon, stir, and serve warm.

Nutritional Values (per serving): Calories: 40 | Total Carbs: 5g | Net Carbs: 4g | Sugar: 1g | Protein: 1g | Fat: 2g | Saturated Fat: 0g | Cholesterol: 0mg | Sodium: 80mg

PINEAPPLE & GINGER IMMUNITY BOOST SMOOTHIE

 PREP TIME: 5 MINS

 COOK TIME: 00 MINS

 SERVING: 2

INGREDIENTS

½ cup fresh pineapple, diced
1 teaspoon grated fresh ginger
1 cup unsweetened coconut water
½ teaspoon lemon juice
3–4 ice cubes

INSTRUCTIONS

1. Peel and dice pineapple, then grate fresh ginger.
2. Add pineapple, ginger, coconut water, and lemon juice to a blender.
3. Blend until smooth, adding ice cubes for a chilled texture.
4. Serve immediately, optionally garnished with a pineapple slice.

Nutritional Values (per serving): Calories: 110 | Total Carbs: 28g | Net Carbs: 26g | Sugar: 20g | Protein: 1g |

Fat: 0g | Saturated Fat: 0g | Cholesterol: 0mg | Sodium: 30mg

TURMERIC GOLDEN MILK WITH ALMOND MILK

 PREP TIME:
5 MINS

 COOK TIME:
5 MINS

 SERVING:
2

INGREDIENTS

1 cup unsweetened almond milk
½ teaspoon ground turmeric
¼ teaspoon ground cinnamon
½ teaspoon honey (optional)
¼ teaspoon black pepper

INSTRUCTIONS

1. Heat almond milk in a saucepan on moderate heat until warm.
2. Whisk in turmeric, cinnamon, black pepper, and honey until well combined.
3. Simmer for 2–3 minutes, stirring occasionally.
4. Serve warm, optionally garnished with a cinnamon stick.

Nutritional Values (per serving): Calories: 90 | Total Carbs: 12g | Net Carbs: 10g | Sugar: 6g | Protein: 2g |
Fat: 4g | Saturated Fat: 1g | Cholesterol: 0mg | Sodium: 50mg

DESSERTS

DARK CHOCOLATE AVOCADO MOUSSE

 PREP TIME: 10 MINS   **COOK TIME:** 00 MINS   **SERVING:** 2

INGREDIENTS

1 ripe avocado
2 tablespoons unsweetened cocoa powder
1 tablespoon honey or maple syrup
¼ teaspoon vanilla extract

2 tablespoons unsweetened almond milk

INSTRUCTIONS

1. Scoop avocado into a blender, then add cocoa powder, honey, and vanilla extract.
2. Blend until smooth, slowly adding almond milk for a creamy texture.
3. Chill in the fridge for 10 minutes to enhance the flavor.
4. Serve topped with berries or chopped nuts if desired.

Nutritional Values (per serving): Calories: 220 | Total Carbs: 24g | Net Carbs: 18g | Sugar: 12g | Protein: 4g | Fat: 14g | Saturated Fat: 3g | Cholesterol: 0mg | Sodium: 40mg

CHIA SEED PUDDING WITH ALMOND MILK & BERRIES

 PREP TIME: 5 MINS

 COOK TIME: 00 MINS

 SERVING: 2

INGREDIENTS

¼ cup chia seeds
1 cup unsweetened almond milk
½ teaspoon vanilla extract
½ cup mixed berries
1 teaspoon honey (optional)

INSTRUCTIONS

1. Mix chia seeds, almond milk, and vanilla extract in a deep-bottom bowl.
2. Stir well, then cover and refrigerate for 2 hours, stirring once halfway.
3. Once thickened, stir again and top with fresh berries.
4. Serve chilled, optionally drizzled with honey for sweetness.

Nutritional Values (per serving):   Calories: 180 | Total Carbs: 22g | Net Carbs: 14g | Sugar: 10g | Protein: 5g |

Fat: 9g | Saturated Fat: 1g | Cholesterol: 0mg | Sodium: 30mg

OATMEAL & BERRY CRUMBLE (LOW SUGAR)

	PREP TIME: 10 MINS		COOK TIME: 20 MINS		SERVING: 2

INGREDIENTS

1 cup mixed berries
¼ teaspoon cinnamon
½ cup rolled oats
1 tablespoon almond flour
1 teaspoon honey or maple syrup
1 teaspoon coconut oil, melted

INSTRUCTIONS

1. Preheat oven to 350°F (175°C). Lightly grease a baking dish.
2. Mix berries with cinnamon and place in the dish.
3. Grab a shallow bowl and mix oats, almond flour, honey, and coconut oil, then sprinkle over the berries.
4. Bake for 20 minutes, until golden and bubbly, then serve warm.

Nutritional Values (per serving): Calories: 220 | Total Carbs: 34g | Net Carbs: 28g | Sugar: 12g | Protein: 6g |

Fat: 7g | Saturated Fat: 1g | Cholesterol: 0mg | Sodium: 50mg

BAKED APPLE WITH CINNAMON & WALNUTS

 PREP TIME:
10 MINS

 COOK TIME:
25 MINS

 SERVING:
2

INGREDIENTS

1 large apple, halved and cored
2 tablespoons chopped walnuts
½ teaspoon cinnamon
1 teaspoon honey or maple syrup
1 teaspoon melted coconut oil

INSTRUCTIONS

1. Preheat oven to 375°F (190°C). Place apple halves in a baking dish.
2. Mix walnuts, cinnamon, honey, and coconut oil, then stuff the apples.
3. Bake for 25 minutes, until tender and caramelized.
4. Serve warm, optionally topped with Greek yogurt.

Nutritional Values (per serving): Calories: 180 | Total Carbs: 30g | Net Carbs: 24g | Sugar: 20g | Protein: 3g |

Fat: 6g | Saturated Fat: 1g | Cholesterol: 0mg | Sodium: 10mg

BANANA & WALNUT ENERGY BITES

 PREP TIME:
10 MINS

 COOK TIME:
20 MINS

 SERVING:
2

INGREDIENTS

1 medium banana, mashed
½ cup rolled oats
¼ cup chopped walnuts
½ teaspoon cinnamon
1 teaspoon honey

INSTRUCTIONS

1. Mash banana in a deep-bottom bowl, then mix in oats, walnuts, cinnamon, and honey.
2. Stir well until combined, then roll into small bite-sized balls.
3. Place on a tray and refrigerate for 20 minutes to firm up.
4. Serve chilled, optionally dusted with extra cinnamon.

Nutritional Values (per serving): Calories: 210 | Total Carbs: 32g | Net Carbs: 26g | Sugar: 14g | Protein: 5g |

Fat: 8g | Saturated Fat: 1g | Cholesterol: 0mg | Sodium: 20mg

GREEK YOGURT WITH HONEY & PISTACHIOS

 **PREP TIME:**
5 MINS

 COOK TIME:
00 MINS

 SERVING:
2

INGREDIENTS

1 cup Greek yogurt (low-fat)
1 teaspoon honey
2 tablespoons chopped pistachios

INSTRUCTIONS

1. Scoop Greek yogurt into serving bowls.
2. Drizzle honey evenly over the yogurt.
3. Sprinkle chopped pistachios on top for crunch.
4. Serve immediately, optionally garnished with a mint leaf.

Nutritional Values (per serving): Calories: 180 | Total Carbs: 18g | Net Carbs: 14g | Sugar: 12g | Protein: 15g
| Fat: 6g | Saturated Fat: 2g | Cholesterol: 10mg | Sodium: 80mg

LOW-SUGAR ALMOND FLOUR BROWNIES

 PREP TIME:
10 MINS

 COOK TIME:
20 MINS

 SERVING:
2

INGREDIENTS

½ cup almond flour
2 tablespoons unsweetened cocoa powder
1 tablespoon honey or maple syrup
1 egg

1 teaspoon vanilla extract

INSTRUCTIONS

1. Preheat oven to 350°F (175°C). Grease a small baking dish.
2. Mix almond flour, cocoa powder, honey, egg, and vanilla extract until smooth.
3. Pour batter into the dish and bake for 18–20 minutes, until set.
4. Let cool, slice into squares, and serve.

Nutritional Values (per serving): Calories: 190 | Total Carbs: 15g | Net Carbs: 12g | Sugar: 8g | Protein: 7g |

Fat: 12g | Saturated Fat: 3g | Cholesterol: 40mg | Sodium: 60mg

FROZEN BANANA & PEANUT BUTTER BITES

 **PREP TIME:**
5 MINS

 COOK TIME:
00 MINS

 SERVING:
2

INGREDIENTS

1 medium banana, sliced
2 tablespoons natural peanut butter

INSTRUCTIONS

1. Place another banana slice on top, making a sandwich.
2. Arrange on a tray and freeze for 1 hour.
3. Serve cold, optionally drizzled with extra peanut butter.

Nutritional Values (per serving):   Calories: 210 | Total Carbs: 28g | Net Carbs: 22g | Sugar: 14g | Protein: 6g |

Fat: 10g | Saturated Fat: 2g | Cholesterol: 0mg | Sodium: 30mg

COCONUT & CHIA SEED PUDDING WITH MANGO

 PREP TIME: 5 MINS   **COOK TIME:** 00 MINS   **SERVING:** 2

INGREDIENTS

¼ cup chia seeds
1 cup light coconut milk
½ cup diced mango
½ teaspoon honey (optional)

INSTRUCTIONS

1. Mix chia seeds and coconut milk in a deep-bottom bowl.
2. Stir well and refrigerate for 2 hours, stirring once halfway.
3. Once thickened, stir again and top with diced mango.
4. Serve chilled, optionally drizzled with honey.

Nutritional Values (per serving): Calories: 230 | Total Carbs: 28g | Net Carbs: 20g | Sugar: 16g | Protein: 5g |

Fat: 12g | Saturated Fat: 6g | Cholesterol: 0mg | Sodium: 35mg

BAKED PEACHES WITH ALMOND BUTTER DRIZZLE

 PREP TIME:
5 MINS

 COOK TIME:
15 MINS

 SERVING:
2

INGREDIENTS

1 large peach, halved and pitted
1 teaspoon almond butter
¼ teaspoon cinnamon
1 teaspoon chopped almonds

INSTRUCTIONS

1. Preheat oven to 375°F (190°C). Place peach halves in a baking dish.
2. Bake for 12–15 minutes, until soft and slightly caramelized.
3. Drizzle with almond butter, then sprinkle with cinnamon and chopped almonds.
4. Serve warm, optionally topped with Greek yogurt.

Nutritional Values (per serving): Calories: 160 | Total Carbs: 24g | Net Carbs: 18g | Sugar: 14g | Protein: 4g |

Fat: 6g | Saturated Fat: 1g | Cholesterol: 0mg | Sodium: 5mg

30-DAY DIET MEAL PLAN & SHOPPING LIST

WEEK 1

	BREAKFAST	LUNCH	DINNER	SNACK
DAY 1	Green Smoothie with Spinach, Banana & Almond Milk	Grilled Chicken Salad with Olive Oil Dressing	Balsamic Glazed Salmon with Steamed Green Beans	Apple Slices with Peanut Butter
DAY 2	Greek Yogurt with Cinnamon & Flaxseeds	Mediterranean Chickpea & Feta Salad	Quinoa-Stuffed Eggplant with Herbs & Parmesan	Handful of Unsalted Almonds & Walnuts
DAY 3	Strawberry & Flaxseed Yogurt Smoothie	Turkey & Spinach Whole-Wheat Wrap	Garlic & Lime Shrimp with Whole-Wheat Couscous	Cucumber Slices with Hummus & Cherry Tomatoes
DAY 4	Almond Butter & Banana Smoothie	Lentil & Chickpea Power Bowl	Grilled Pork Tenderloin with Mashed Cauliflower	Roasted Chickpeas with Smoked Paprika
DAY 5	Almond Milk Latte with Whole-Wheat Crackers	Baked Salmon with Roasted Vegetables	Turkey Chili with Black Beans & Avocado	Greek Yogurt with Honey & Pistachios
DAY 6	Berry & Chia Protein Smoothie	Whole-Wheat Pasta with Spinach, Olive Oil & Garlic	Grilled Chicken with Roasted Sweet Potatoes	Baked Sweet Potato Fries with Garlic & Herbs
DAY 7	Pineapple & Ginger Immunity Boost Smoothie	Quinoa & Black Bean Salad with Lime Dressing	Baked Cod with Lemon & Garlic	Hard-Boiled Eggs with Whole-Grain Crackers

WEEK 1 SHOPPING LIST

PROTEINS & DAIRY
- [ ] Chicken breasts (4 boneless, skinless)
- [ ] Salmon fillets (2, 4 oz each)
- [ ] Lean beef (6 oz, sliced)
- [ ] Ground turkey (½ pound)
- [ ] Large shrimp (10, peeled & deveined)
- [ ] Eggs (4 large)
- [ ] Low-fat cottage cheese (1 cup)
- [ ] Greek yogurt (1 cup)
- [ ] Feta cheese (¼ cup)
- [ ] Plant-based protein powder (½ scoop)

Grains & Legumes
- [ ] Whole-wheat pasta (1 cup)
- [ ] Brown rice (½ cup dry)
- [ ] Quinoa (½ cup dry)
- [ ] Lentils (½ cup dry)
- [ ] Chickpeas (½ cup dry, soaked overnight)
- [ ] Whole-wheat couscous (½ cup dry)
- [ ] Kidney beans (½ cup dry, soaked overnight)
- [ ] Whole-wheat crackers (8)
- [ ] Whole-wheat tortillas (2)
- [ ] Rolled oats (½ cup)

Vegetables & Fruits
- [ ] Cucumber (1 small)
- [ ] Fresh spinach (1 cup)
- [ ] Mixed greens (2 cups)
- [ ] Cherry tomatoes (1 cup)
- [ ] Carrots (1 cup, diced)
- [ ] Celery (½ cup, diced)
- [ ] Zucchini (½ cup, diced)
- [ ] Bell peppers (½ cup, diced)
- [ ] Broccoli florets (1 cup)
- [ ] Red onion (½ cup, finely chopped)
- [ ] Blueberries (½ cup)
- [ ] Apple (1 medium)
- [ ] Banana (1 medium)
- [ ] Avocado (½)
- [ ] Strawberries (½ cup)

Pantry & Condiments
- [ ] Olive oil
- [ ] Balsamic vinegar
- [ ] Lemon juice
- [ ] Oregano
- [ ] Cumin
- [ ] Minced garlic
- [ ] Honey
- [ ] Vanilla extract

WEEK 2

	BREAKFAST	LUNCH	DINNER	SNACK
DAY 1	Low-Fat Cottage Cheese with Blueberries	Whole-Wheat Crackers with Avocado & Feta	Stuffed Bell Peppers with Ground Turkey & Quinoa	Handful of Unsalted Almonds & Walnuts
DAY 2	DASH Diet Omelet with Spinach & Feta	Roasted Brussels Sprouts & Quinoa with Almonds	Lean Beef Stir-Fry with Brown Rice & Peppers	Greek Yogurt with Cinnamon & Flaxseeds
DAY 3	Watermelon & Coconut Water Refresher	Mediterranean Chickpea & Spinach Stew	Roasted Chicken with Roasted Vegetables	Baked Sweet Potato Fries with Garlic & Herbs
DAY 4	Chia Seed Pudding with Almond Milk & Berries	Hummus with Carrot & Cucumber Sticks	Grilled Salmon with Mango Salsa & Brown Rice	Apple Slices with Peanut Butter
DAY 5	Turmeric Golden Milk with Almond Milk	Tofu & Broccoli Stir-Fry with Cashews	Sweet Potato & Black Bean Enchiladas	Roasted Chickpeas with Smoked Paprika
DAY 6	Dark Chocolate Avocado Mousse	Quinoa & Black Bean Salad with Lime Dressing	Balsamic Glazed Chicken with Roasted Brussels Sprouts	Banana & Walnut Energy Bites
DAY 7	Greek Yogurt with Honey & Pistachios	Spiced Lentil & Roasted Cauliflower Bowl	Turkey Meatballs with Whole-Wheat Spaghetti	Frozen Banana & Peanut Butter Bites

WEEK 2 SHOPPING LIST

Proteins & Dairy
- [ ] Chicken breasts (4 boneless, skinless)
- [ ] Cod fillets (2, 4 oz each)
- [ ] Ground turkey (½ pound)
- [ ] Pork tenderloin (6 oz)
- [ ] Feta cheese (½ cup, crumbled)
- [ ] Greek yogurt (1 cup)
- [ ] Almond butter (2 tablespoons)

Grains & Legumes
- [ ] Whole-wheat pasta (1 cup)
- [ ] Black beans (½ cup dry, soaked overnight)
- [ ] Quinoa (½ cup dry)
- [ ] Rolled oats (½ cup)
- [ ] Almond flour (½ cup)
- [ ] Cashews (¼ cup, raw)
- [ ] Walnuts (¼ cup, chopped)

Vegetables & Fruits
- [ ] Cucumber (1 small)
- [ ] Fresh spinach (1 cup)
- [ ] Tomatoes (½ cup, diced)
- [ ] Sweet potato (1 medium)
- [ ] Peach (1 small)
- [ ] Banana (1 medium)
- [ ] Mango (½ cup, diced)

Pantry & Condiments
- [ ] Olive oil
- [ ] Lime juice
- [ ] Cinnamon
- [ ] Turmeric
- [ ] Basil
- [ ] Chia seeds
- Chili powder

WEEK 3

	BREAKFAST	LUNCH	DINNER	DESSERT
DAY 1	Green Smoothie with Spinach, Banana & Almond Milk	Whole-Wheat Pasta with Roasted Vegetables & Feta	Garlic & Lime Shrimp with Whole-Wheat Couscous	Chia Seed Pudding with Almond Milk & Berries
DAY 2	Greek Yogurt with Cinnamon & Flaxseeds	Quinoa & Black Bean Salad with Lime Dressing	Grilled Chicken with Roasted Sweet Potatoes	Dark Chocolate Avocado Mousse
DAY 3	Pineapple & Ginger Immunity Boost Smoothie	Balsamic Glazed Salmon with Steamed Green Beans	Roasted Brussels Sprouts & Quinoa with Almonds	Low-Sugar Almond Flour Brownies
DAY 4	Strawberry & Flaxseed Yogurt Smoothie	Lentil & Kale Stew with Garlic & Herbs	Mediterranean-Style Stuffed Peppers	Baked Apple with Cinnamon & Walnuts
DAY 5	Greek Yogurt with Honey & Pistachios	Hummus & Roasted Veggie Pita Pocket	Grilled Salmon with Mango Salsa & Brown Rice	Coconut & Chia Seed Pudding with Mango
DAY 6	Almond Butter & Banana Smoothie	Quinoa & Black Bean Chili	Lean Beef Stir-Fry with Brown Rice & Peppers	Oatmeal & Berry Crumble (Low Sugar)
DAY 7	Almond Milk Latte with Whole-Wheat Crackers	Spiced Sweet Potato & Carrot Soup	Baked Tilapia with Garlic & Roasted Carrots	Frozen Banana & Peanut Butter Bites

WEEK 3 SHOPPING LIST

Proteins & Dairy
- [ ] Chicken thighs (2, bone-in)
- [ ] Eggs (4 large)
- [ ] Low-fat cottage cheese (1 cup)
- [ ] Salmon fillets (2, 4 oz each)
- [ ] Ground turkey (½ pound)
- [ ] Parmesan cheese (¼ cup, shredded)

Grains & Legumes
- [ ] Lentils (½ cup dry)
- [ ] Black beans (½ cup dry, soaked overnight)
- [ ] Quinoa (½ cup dry)
- [ ] Wild rice (½ cup dry)
- [ ] Sliced almonds (¼ cup)
- [ ] Whole-wheat crackers (8)
- [ ] Whole-wheat tortillas (2)

Vegetables & Fruits
- [ ] Zucchini (1 small)
- [ ] Bell peppers (½ cup, diced)
- [ ] Fresh spinach (1 cup)
- [ ] Tomatoes (½ cup, diced)
- [ ] Sweet potato (1 medium)
- [ ] Apple (1 large)
- [ ] Cucumber (1 small)

Pantry & Condiments
- [ ] Olive oil
- [ ] Cumin
- [ ] Smoked paprika
- [ ] Ground cinnamon

WEEK 4

	BREAKFAST	LUNCH	DINNER	DESSERT
DAY 1	Greek Yogurt with Cinnamon & Flaxseeds	Hummus & Roasted Veggie Pita Pocket	Roasted Brussels Sprouts & Quinoa with Almonds	Dark Chocolate Avocado Mousse
DAY 2	Watermelon & Coconut Water Refresher	Spiced Lentil & Roasted Cauliflower Bowl	Garlic & Lime Shrimp with Whole-Wheat Couscous	Baked Peaches with Almond Butter Drizzle
DAY 3	Chia Seed Pudding with Almond Milk & Berries	Turkey & Spinach Whole-Wheat Wrap	Turkey Meatballs with Whole-Wheat Spaghetti	Banana & Walnut Energy Bites
DAY 4	Pineapple & Ginger Immunity Boost Smoothie	Mediterranean Chickpea & Spinach Stew	Lean Beef Stir-Fry with Brown Rice & Peppers	Low-Sugar Almond Flour Brownies
DAY 5	Cottage Cheese with Blueberries	Baked Salmon with Roasted Vegetables	Grilled Chicken with Roasted Sweet Potatoes	Baked Apple with Cinnamon & Walnuts
DAY 6	Low-Fat Cottage Cheese with Blueberries	Avocado & Turkey Lettuce Wraps	Grilled Chicken with Roasted Sweet Potatoes	Baked Apple with Cinnamon & Walnuts
DAY 7	Almond Butter & Banana Smoothie	Quinoa & Black Bean Chili	Grilled Salmon with Mango Salsa & Brown Rice	Coconut & Chia Seed Pudding with Mango

WEEK 4 SHOPPING LIST

Proteins & Dairy
- [ ] Chicken breasts (2 boneless, skinless)
- [ ] Salmon fillets (2, 4 oz each)
- [ ] Ground turkey (½ pound)
- [ ] Eggs (4 large)
- [ ] Greek yogurt (1 cup)
- [ ] Feta cheese (¼ cup, crumbled)

Grains & Legumes
- [ ] Lentils (½ cup dry)
- [ ] Black beans (½ cup dry, soaked overnight)
- [ ] Quinoa (½ cup dry)
- [ ] Rolled oats (½ cup)
- [ ] Whole-wheat pasta (½ cup)
- [ ] Almond flour (½ cup)

Vegetables & Fruits
- [ ] Banana (1 medium)
- [ ] Strawberries (½ cup)
- [ ] Mango (½ cup, diced)
- [ ] Sweet potato (1 medium)
- [ ] Peach (1 small)
- [ ] Fresh spinach (1 cup)

Pantry & Condiments
- [ ] Olive oil
- [ ] Balsamic vinegar
- [ ] Honey
- [ ] Ground cinnamon
- [ ] Turmeric
- [ ] Oregano

INDEX

A

Almond Butter & Banana Smoothie 99
Apple Slices with Peanut Butter 86
Avocado Toast with Egg on Whole-Wheat Bread 13
Avocado & Turkey Lettuce Wraps 43

B

Baked Apple Oatmeal Bars 28
Baked Apple with Cinnamon & Walnuts 109
Baked Cod with Lemon & Garlic 54
Baked Peaches with Almond Butter Drizzle 115
Baked Salmon with Roasted Vegetables 37
Baked Sweet Potato Fries with Garlic & Herbs 89
Baked Tilapia with Garlic & Roasted Carrots 71
Balsamic Glazed Chicken with Roasted Brussels Sprouts 46
Balsamic Glazed Salmon with Steamed Green Beans 57
Banana & Chia Seed Breakfast Bowl 14
Banana & Walnut Energy Bites 110
Berry & Chia Protein Smoothie 96
Brown Rice & Grilled Tofu Stir-Fry 42

C

Chia Seed Pudding with Almond Milk & Berries 107
Chicken & Brown Rice Soup (Low-Sodium) 77
Coconut & Chia Seed Pudding with Mango 114
Coconut Curry Lentil Soup 82
Cottage Cheese with Walnuts & Cinnamon 17
Cucumber & Mint Hydration Drink 98
Cucumber Slices with Hummus & Cherry Tomatoes 92

D

Dark Chocolate Avocado Mousse 106

E

Egg Salad on Whole-Grain Toast (Low Mayo) 39

F

Frozen Banana & Peanut Butter Bites 113

G

Garlic & Lime Shrimp with Whole-Wheat Couscous 60
Greek Yogurt with Cinnamon & Flaxseeds 91
Greek Yogurt with Honey & Pistachios 111
Greek Yogurt with Nuts & Honey 12
Green Smoothie with Spinach, Banana & Almond Milk 95
Grilled Chicken Salad with Olive Oil Dressing 32
Grilled Chicken with Roasted Sweet Potatoes 52
Grilled Pork Tenderloin with Mashed Cauliflower 63
Grilled Salmon with Mango Salsa & Brown Rice 67
Grilled Shrimp with Brown Rice & Steamed Broccoli 38
Grilled Veggie & Hummus Whole-Wheat Wrap 48

H

Handful of Unsalted Almonds & Walnuts 85
Hard-Boiled Eggs with Whole-Grain Crackers 29, 93
Hearty Vegetable Soup with Lentils 73
High-Protein Chia Pudding with Nuts & Seeds 24
Hummus & Roasted Veggie Pita Pocket 40
Hummus with Carrot & Cucumber Sticks 84

L

Lean Beef Stir-Fry with Brown Rice & Peppers 62
Lemon Herb Baked Cod with Asparagus 44
Lentil & Chickpea Power Bowl 33
Lentil & Kale Stew with Garlic & Herbs 76

Low-Fat Cottage Cheese with Blueberries 87
Low-Sodium Breakfast Burrito (Egg, Avocado & Beans) 22
Low-Sodium Herb Roasted Chicken with Quinoa Pilaf 59
Low-Sodium Minestrone with Whole-Grain Pasta 74
Low-Sodium Tomato Juice Blend 97
Low-Sugar Almond Flour Brownies 112
Low-Sugar Almond Milk Latte 102

M

Mediterranean Chickpea & Feta Salad 36
Mediterranean Chickpea & Spinach Stew 79
Mediterranean-Style Stuffed Peppers 56

O

Oatmeal & Berry Crumble (Low Sugar) 108
Oatmeal with Berries & Almonds 11
Oatmeal with Flaxseeds & Cinnamon 27

P

Peanut Butter & Banana on Whole-Grain Toast 19
Pineapple & Ginger Immunity Boost Smoothie 103

Q

Quinoa & Black Bean Chili soup 81
Quinoa & Black Bean Salad with Lime Dressing 34
Quinoa Breakfast Bowl with Almonds & Raisins 21
Quinoa-Stuffed Eggplant with Herbs & Parmesan 58

R

Roasted Brussels Sprouts & Quinoa with Almonds 70
Roasted Chicken with Roasted Vegetables 65
Roasted Chickpeas with Smoked Paprika 88
Roasted Red Pepper & Tomato Soup 80

S

Scrambled Egg Whites with Spinach & Feta 15
Spiced Lentil & Roasted Cauliflower Bowl 49
Spiced Sweet Potato & Carrot Soup 78
Spinach & Grilled Chicken Stuffed Sweet Potato 41
Spinach & Mushroom Breakfast Wrap 26
Stir-Fried Tofu with Brown Rice & Vegetables 53
Strawberry & Flaxseed Yogurt Smoothie 100
Stuffed Acorn Squash with Wild Rice & Nuts 69
Stuffed Bell Peppers with Ground Turkey & Quinoa 47
Sweet Potato & Black Bean Breakfast Hash 20
Sweet Potato & Black Bean Enchiladas (Low-Sodium) 64

T

Tofu & Broccoli Stir-Fry with Cashews 66
Tomato & Basil Scrambled Eggs on Whole-Wheat Toast 25
Tomato Basil Soup with Quinoa 75
Turkey Chili with Black Beans & Avocado 55
Turkey Meatballs with Whole-Wheat Spaghetti 68
Turkey & Spinach Whole-Wheat Wrap 35
Turmeric Golden Milk with Almond Milk 104

V

Vegetable & Cheese Omelet 18

W

Watermelon & Coconut Water Refresher 101
Whole-Grain English Muffin with Almond Butter 23
Whole-Wheat Crackers with Avocado & Feta 90
Whole-Wheat Pancakes with Fresh Berries 16
Whole-Wheat Pasta with Roasted Vegetables & Feta 45
Whole-Wheat Pasta with Spinach, Olive Oil & Garlic 61

Z

Zucchini & Cheese Breakfast Muffins 30
Zucchini Noodles with Pesto & Grilled Chicken 50